When the Moment Chooses You

When the Moment Chooses You
From Silence to Strength: A Nurse Leader's Journey
Find Your Voice, Unleash Your Impact

Copyright © 2025 Charlene Johnson. All rights reserved.

All rights reserved. No part of this book shall be reproduced, stored in a retrieval system, or transmitted by any means; electronic, mechanical, photocopying, recording or otherwise, without written permission from the publisher, except for providing a direct quote and providing reference.

For quantity discounts, please contact info@wellnesswhispererconsulting.com

ISBN:
Paperback: 979-8-9926794-0-3
Hardcover: 979-8-9926794-1-0
Ebook: 979-8-9926794-2-7

Editing: Robin Steinweg • RobinSteinweg.wixsite.com/my-site-1 | RobinSteinweg.com

Design: Bookable Media • BookableMedia.com

Images: Adobe Stock

Photography: Ammala Rattana, APICTURE & CO

When the Moment Chooses You

From Silence to Strength: A Nurse Leader's Journey

Find Your Voice, Unleash Your Impact

CHARLENE JOHNSON, MSN, RN

THE NURSE WHISPERER

YOUR GIFT FROM COACH CHARLENE

The Resilient You

Unlocking the Path to Unshakable Resilience

Thank you for choosing to embark on this transformative journey with me!

As a heartfelt appreciation, enjoy this complimentary training on **"The Resilient You: Unlocking the Path to Unshakable Resilience."** This empowering toolkit will enable you to:

» **Master stress effectively**, reclaiming emotional energy even amidst life's toughest challenge.

» **Break free from burnout**, rediscovering joy, passion, and renewed purpose in your professional and personal life.

» **Build unshakable resilience**, empowering you to boldly step into your moments of destiny and create lasting impact.

WATCH NOW

Enjoy your gift:
WellnessWhispererConsulting.com/gift

What Readers are Saying

This book resonated in the deepest part of my heart. In *When the Moment Chooses You*, Coach Charlene provides insights on connecting with your inner voice—the GPS of your soul—steering you along the path uniquely chosen and tailored for you. As she says, "A single moment can move us into a destiny greater than we could ever imagine." Open your heart as you read and allow *this moment* and the heartfelt intentions of its author to choose you!

Joellen Sutterfield
Vice President Clinical Education Management

Coach Charlene's book, *When the Moment Chooses You*, provides a guide to recognize the key moments in your life which are catalysts to your destiny. Her experience, empathy, and grace; commitment, passion, and wisdom light the way for us to seize those moments when we are called beyond ourselves to a future where everyone is seen, heard and valued. We discover resilience to find and share our voice so we too can light the way for others. Thank you, Charlene.

Jan Anderson, EdD, RN, AHN-BC, Caritas Coach
Watson Caring Science Institute Consultant

The truth, beauty, and love in *When the Moment Chooses You* are an invitation to enter an experience of self-discovery overflowing with illumination, opportunity, and hope. Coach Charlene's words are rich with insight and practical tools. You will find a roadmap to discover the key moments that choose you, and an awareness of how we impact each other through the choices we make. This is a book so full of treasure, you will want to return to it again and again.

Kathy Douglas, Co-founder, CEO
The Nursing Way

I savored each word of Charlene's book, soaking up wisdom from one who lives and leads with authenticity, integrity, and a higher purpose. In each chapter Charlene offers key questions for reflection, action, and takeaways to guide the many paradigm shifts. I highly recommend *When the Moment Chooses You* as a guide to your journey of personal transformation.

Tera Eng, Regional Director

Coach Charlene's *When the Moment Chooses You* opens with a deeply personal reflection on the unpredictable nature of life's moments, particularly in the face of adversity and societal turmoil. From the first paragraph she establishes an unfiltered, heartfelt connection with her audience. For those seeking a book that not only acknowledges the hardships of the past but encourages present resilience, action, and healing, *When the Moment Chooses You* will prove a powerful and transformative read.

Dr. Nicole Barnett, CEO
Planned Parenthood Northern California

I was deeply moved by this powerful, wisdom-filled book in which Coach Charlene heartfully illustrates what it means to be a courageous nurse. Her insights on embracing the key moments in life with love, authenticity, and compassion are uplifting and transformative. *When the Moment Chooses You* is a call to bravery, urging us to embody our roles with grace and grit. We are guided and inspired to rediscover our purpose.

Erica D. Hooper, DNP, RN, CNS, CNL, PHN

As I read *When the Moment Chooses You*, it stirred something deep within—provoked the voice inside me to step out of the shadows. I wanted the words to fill me so I could release and speak them to others. As founder, creator, and CEO of Mahogany Life Empowerment Church and of The Price of Safety Inc., I will implement this book in our companys' orientation and introductory trainings. It will build people of God who embody and cultivate love, positively impacting everyone they encounter. Written with the pen of human experience, this book is the perfect introduction to what happens when The Moment chooses you. Congratulations, Coach Charlene, on a beautifully-crafted labor of love.

Stephaine Price, CEO of Mahogany Life Empowerment Church
and CEO of The Price of Safety Inc.

Acknowledgments

To my Family: First and foremost, to my husband, Don—thank you for your unwavering love and support. Your prayers, words of life, and steadfast presence have covered me, uplifted me, and helped me become all that God has destined me to be. To my children Malcolm, Dominique, and Nehemiah, you are my heartbeat and the reason I do what I do. Being your mother is such an honor, and I will forever be your cheerleader and always in your corner. I pray that you will always have the courage to keep following your dream no matter what life throws your way.

To Coach Al and Hattie Hollingsworth, my Spiritual Midwives, who challenged me, encouraged me, and pushed me to birth my dreams and the desires of my heart—thank you for believing in me.

Special thank you to Dr. Jean Watson, the visionary of Caring Science who was bold enough to be disruptive and believe that we can change the world with love.

To all the leaders at KP who believed in me, saw me, and sponsored me, allowing my gift to shine. I am forever grateful. A special thank you to **Linda Ackerman** and **Tera Eng**, whose sponsorship and belief in me opened doors for me to share my voice and find my community.

Above all, to **my Lord and Savior, Jesus Christ**—the One whose presence enables me to forgive quickly, love deeply, and be a light in the midst of darkness.

---

*I also dedicate this book to my wonderful parents,
James and Fannie Johnson and my two sisters, Jackie and Charmaine Johnson
who are no longer with us. Mom and Dad, I will continue to carry
your legacy of love for God and love for humanity forever.*

Contents

Preface xi

Foreword xii

Introduction xv

Chapter 1: A Moment to Reflect
The Unpredictable Nature of Life's Moments 1

Chapter 2: A Moment to Embrace
Finding Courage in Uncertainty 9

Chapter 3: A Moment to Awaken
Recognizing the Whispers 19

Chapter 4: A Moment to Overcome
Navigating Life's Challenges with Resilience 25

Chapter 5: A Moment to Align
Discovering Serendipity and Synchronicity 31

Chapter 6: A Moment to Transform
Embracing Personal Growth and Change 47

Chapter 7: A Moment to Prepare
Being Ready When Your Moment Chooses You! 53

Chapter 8: A Moment to Leap
Launching Out into the Deep and Finding Your Destiny 69

Chapter 9: A Moment to Share
Wisdom Jewel from a Black Nurse Leader's Journey 77

A Final Word from Coach Charlene	85
Conclusion	87
Step Into Your Moment	88
About the Author	91
With Love and Appreciation!	93
Heartfelt Gratitude	95
When Silence is No Longer Safety	96

Preface

A Word from Coach Charlene

As I reflect on the journey that led to the creation of this book, I am reminded of the countless moments—some profound, some fleeting—which have shaped my path as a nurse leader and human being. Each moment, like a brushstroke on the canvas of my life, has left its mark, guiding me to greater self-discovery, resilience, and purpose.

When the Moment Chooses You is more than just a collection of stories. It is a testament to the power of embracing the unexpected, finding strength in adversity, and discovering one's voice in the face of silence. In these pages, I invite you to join me on a journey of exploration and empowerment—a journey that transcends the boundaries of healthcare leadership and speaks to the universal human experience of growth, transformation, and self-realization.

Through personal anecdotes, reflections, and wisdom gleaned from years of navigating the complexities of healthcare, I hope to illuminate the path to authentic leadership, meaningful change, and collective empowerment. From moments of uncertainty and doubt to moments of clarity and conviction, each chapter offers insights and lessons learned, serving as guideposts for those embarking on their own journey of self-discovery and leadership.

It is my sincere hope that this book serves as a source of inspiration, encouragement, and empowerment for nurses, leaders, and changemakers alike. May it spark conversations, ignite passions, and awaken the inner leader within each reader, reminding us of the profound impact we can have when we allow the moment to choose us.

Thank you for embarking on this journey with me.

Warm regards,
Coach Charlene

Foreword

Simon T. Bailey, Amplifier of Brilliance

Speaker, Author, Master Life Coach

You are holding a book that is a care package for the soul, a guide through the cocoon of uncertainty into the freedom of possibility. In these pages, Charlene masterfully coaches us to embrace the present moment—not as something to fear, but as the very place where transformation begins. Like a butterfly emerging from its chrysalis, we are invited to spread our wings and step boldly into what's next.

Charlene's words are more than wisdom. They are wind beneath our wings. Gently yet powerfully she guides us through the phases of our journey. She helps us crawl in the moment, walk toward the moment, and ultimately run into the moment with purpose and confidence. Through her insights, we find permission to reclaim our voice, to embrace the unexpected intersections of life, and to see every encounter with the future as an opportunity to rise.

As I turned the pages, I found myself having Aha moments again and again—proof that this is not just a book, it is a catalyst for reflection, growth, and action. Charlene reminds us that the rearview mirror of yesterday may hold pain, but the windshield ahead reveals a brilliant future. She teaches us that compounded moments create momentum, and momentum shapes our tomorrow.

This book is a gift. It is an invitation. And most importantly, it is a call to step forward—ready, willing, and prepared for the brilliance that awaits.

Let the journey begin.

Foreword

Jean Watson, PhD, RN, AHN-BC, FAAN, LL(AAN)

Founder of Watson Caring Science Institute

Charlene Johnson's book *When the Moment Chooses You* reveals her inner and outer personal journey in professional nursing to serve and to lead from the silent calling within. As you enter into and accept this powerful invitation and its personal messages, you will cross a dynamic threshold of awakening to spirit and strength.

Core insights and lessons of personal spiritual growth await you to:

- » Reflect
- » Embrace
- » Awaken
- » Overcome
- » Align
- » Transform
- » Prepare
- » Leap
- » Share

Charlene offers wisdom from personal, anecdotal, and even doubt-filled moments. She goes beyond herself to provide readers a springboard to self-discovery and passion. These storied moments embrace the unexpected as a turning point to navigate complex situations: situations which whisper, *The moment is choosing you to rise and shine as the star you already are.* You pave the way for others to follow.

Faced with upheaval and chaotic changes in self, healthcare systems, and society, Coach Charlene provides a personal and professional refuge and guide. It lifts you to a higher version of your self. It challenges systems. Then we hear the whisper of our inner wisdom and know:

The Moment Has Chosen YOU!

Introduction

You know, no one could have foreseen the whirlwind that was 2020—a year of unprecedented change and division. It felt like we were battling not just one, but multiple pandemics. The invisible enemy, COVID-19, infiltrated our cities and our world, bringing with it fear and uncertainty. Simultaneously, racial unrest reignited across the nation, exposing deep-rooted injustice and division. And in it all, our sense of certainty and freedom seemed to slip away, plunging us into uncharted territory.

It was a year of sobering moments, defining moments that tested our humanity to its very core. As a nurse, I've encountered many of these moments throughout my career—times when I questioned whether I had chosen the right path. But amid the chaos and doubt, I found my voice. And now I'm ready to share my story with the world.

The year 2020 served as a stark reminder of the power of moments—moments that call us to disrupt, dismantle, change, and transform. Whether from within ourselves or within the systems we're a part of, we each have the power to bring about change. We recognize those moments that beckon us to step forward, respond, and make a difference. So, I urge you to heed the call of those moments in your own life. Embrace them, for they hold the potential to reshape not only your world but the world around you.

CHAPTER 1

A Moment to Reflect

The Unpredictable Nature of Life's Moments

> *"In the face of adversity, we discover our true strength. With courage as our guide and compassion as our fuel, we transform pain into power and darkness into light. This is not just our journey. It's our legacy of inspiration, empowerment, and transformation."*
>
> —*Coach Charlene*

During one of the worst pandemics ever, May 2020, the world witnessed another Black man, George Floyd, being subdued to the point of death. To set context, we had just witnessed two other deaths: Ahmaud Arbery, a twenty-five-year-old Black man jogging in February not far from his home; and Breonna Taylor, a twenty-six-year-old medical worker who was killed after forced entry into her home.

The pain and deep hurt I felt yet again was more than words can express. I was thankful I was on vacation at the time of this particular incident because the impact of what I saw struck in me a sad reality that this would not be the last atrocity we would witness. The trauma of seeing young Black men and women killed before my eyes made me think of a lot of things. *This is someone's son, husband, brother, nephew, father, and so on, and so on.* These feelings became so overwhelming I couldn't bear it alone. I went to the only entity I knew could support me in a time like this—my Creator God Himself, the one who designed and crafted me. The shock and disarray of witnessing this modern-day lynching was so traumatic, it was almost too much to absorb. Every time a death of this nature takes place it takes my breath away and triggers traumatic emotions in me as a person of color. Another life with so much potential aborted way too soon.

Loss, sickness, hatred, political division, racial tension, and unrest consumed our cities as the world joined hands to say enough is enough. As a Black nurse leader, my heart was extremely heavy as we were already experiencing the crisis of the COVID-19 surge for the first time, and now we added another pandemic, *systemic racism,* which had already been woven into the fabric of our society for as long as I can remember. Wait, let's not forget to mention we also had to deal with our own personal pandemics such as loss of family, loss of finances, loss of connection, and loss of control we once knew. Loss, loss, loss.

The numbness that came over me as a Black leader was palpable. *I'm tired. I'm not okay. I'm just plain exhausted.* This moment was even heavier for me because I intuitively knew my peers, friends, and employees would reach out to me because I was one of the few Black nurse leaders at the time. I knew in a situation like this, others would be seeking answers, or just some type of normalcy. As a Black person, I understood how difficult it was for Blacks to continue to show up and perform duties while being wounded by witnessing yet another one of our brothers being murdered. We had to show up while hearing all of the insensitive comments and opinions of those not affected, which in and of itself was traumatizing. It was like trying to convince others that yes, we may live in the same neighborhood, but our house—our Black community—is literally on fire, and we must focus all of our attention on that one house to extinguish the fire. We need our allies and everyone to offer support, even if they don't know what to do!

As I cried out in prayer and searched for how to keep moving forward amid the pain in this moment, I heard a soft, gentle voice speak to my spirit: *"What you do in this moment will determine your destiny and dictate your future!"*

What powerful, life-giving words! God spoke to my spirit to commission me to stop being silent and speak up. He wanted me to move from anger and frustration to action and impact. Once I heard those words, my natural tears stopped, the pain began to subside, my tears turned into an internal cry, and the next steps became quite clear. It was time for me to choose to be a light in the midst of this darkness, and to allow the pain to become fuel for my next steps. It was time for me to be a disruptor and a part of the solution. It was time to break my silence and share my stories of racism experienced throughout my career with my organization as a bridge to bring perspective, awareness, and healing. Dr. Martin Luther King once said, "Our lives begin to end the day we become silent about things that matter!" Finally, after multiple years of subtle microaggression, insensitive remarks, devaluation, and feeling unseen, I shattered the silence and awakened my voice.

Let's revisit the life-altering statement that stirred me into action: "What I do in this moment will determine my destiny and dictate my future!" Life inevitably throws choices our way, especially in the aftermath of traumatic events. At that pivotal juncture, I realized I had three options: I could either remain ensnared in the clutches of trauma, rendering myself powerless; I could confront the pain head-on; or I could decide to do nothing.

By understanding the emotions associated with it and letting them pass through me, I could transform this adversity into intentional action, a force for making a difference. I urge you to view every moment of trauma, frustration or disappointment as a potential steppingstone to triumph. Embrace the challenges, master your emotions, and let them guide you to purposeful action—even if it causes you to speak up and be disruptive. In doing so, you can turn adversity into a catalyst for positive transformation.

A moment to unleash courage and find your voice.

You may ask, "Why didn't you speak up sooner? Why did it take so long to say something?" For many who are marginalized, the answer is clear and deeply understood. Systemic racism is not a relic of the past. It is woven into the fabric of our world and institutions, confronting us daily. Many of us carry the heavy responsibility of being the breadwinners for our families, and the stakes are high. Speaking up often means risking backlash, be it professional, personal, or both. And this fear keeps many voices silent.

Speaking up is never an easy task, especially when you're in the minority and have never been given the opportunity—or the space—to do so. Finding your voice amid oppression is not instinctive. It demands both courage and conviction. Often these moments call to you, stirring something so deep within your soul it can no longer be ignored. The courage to speak out against injustice is nothing short of an act of bravery. It is a stand for ethical principles, equity, and the well-being of those who have been silenced. It means choosing to rise in the face of wrongdoing, even when it is uncomfortable or dangerous to do so.

In a world where silence so often perpetuates harm, speaking up becomes a guiding light in the darkness. It's a deliberate choice to lend your voice to the voiceless, to champion the rights of those who've been overlooked, and to challenge a status quo that thrives on inequality. This kind of courage isn't born from anger or impulsiveness. It is rooted in empathy, integrity, and an unyielding commitment to justice and fairness. It's an understanding that when we turn a blind eye to injustice, we allow it to grow stronger. Therefore, speaking up becomes not just a personal choice but a moral obligation—your voice becomes a catalyst for change—for the love of humanity.

But here's the truth: speaking up requires you to confront your own fears. It means acknowledging the risks—criticism, backlash, or even personal loss—and stepping forward anyway. It is recognizing that the discomfort you may feel pales in comparison to the suffering endured by those directly affected by the injustice.

True courage shines when you educate yourself on the issue, when you take the time to gather the facts, and engage in meaningful dialogue. Armed with knowledge, compassion, and experience, you address the injustice with conviction and purpose. You understand your voice carries weight, and in every conversation—whether it be in public, on social media, or in private—you hold the power to shift perspectives. Your words become a powerful force of truth. They push against the forces of oppression and inequality.

Even in the face of resistance your courage holds steady. You remain calm, articulate, and composed, even when disagreement and dissent surround you. This unshakable resolve showcases the depth of your commitment to justice.

Your courage doesn't stop at raising awareness. It sparks action. You inspire others to stand alongside you, forging a movement for a fairer world. Your unwavering stance emboldens those who've felt voiceless to join the chorus of change.

In time, your decision to speak up leaves a lasting imprint. It contributes to a more just, equitable, and compassionate society, where the voices of the oppressed are amplified and systemic wrongs are dismantled. The courage to speak up against injustice is more than just correcting a wrong. It is a testament to the resilience of the human spirit and a glimmer of possibility for a better, brighter future. It is a reminder that every voice, no matter how small, holds the potential for extraordinary change.

Now that you understand the power of your voice, I leave you with this question: *Will you find your voice and speak? The world is waiting to hear from you.*

Summary

Chapter 1, "A Moment to Reflect," explores the transformative power of adversity and the defining moments that call us to action. Against the backdrop of personal and societal crises—systemic racism and the COVID-19 pandemic—Coach Charlene reflects on her own awakening. This was the moment that chose her. A time when the world seemed to crumble under the weight of loss, inequity, and division. It was a moment of reckoning, where silence was no longer an option, and the whispers of her heart demanded she rise with courage and conviction.

With raw vulnerability, she shares her journey of confronting trauma and breaking the silence to speak up for justice, equity, and humanity. Her story illuminates the invisible scars left by a lifetime of judgment and devaluation, scars she chose to address through faith, inner healing, and resilience. Coach Charlene challenges readers to see their own adversity as an opportunity to find strength, embrace their voice, and create meaningful change.

Now is the time to awaken the power within you, to transform pain into purpose, and to step boldly into your own moment of truth.

Key Takeaways

- » **Resilience:** Adversity reveals our innate strength and resilience, helping us navigate challenges with grace.
- » **Transformation:** Finding purpose in pain empowers us to drive positive change in our communities.
- » **Solidarity:** Speaking up against injustice creates change that inspires collective action.

Reflective Questions

1. How have your own experiences of adversity shaped your understanding of resilience and courage?
2. What fears have held you back from addressing systemic issues in your personal or professional life?
3. How can your voice inspire a culture of understanding, respect, and compassion in the spaces you influence?

Reflective Questions

Reflective Questions

CHAPTER 2

A Moment to Embrace

Finding Courage in Uncertainty

> *"Embrace uncertainty as the canvas upon which your greatest adventures are painted. It is in the unknown that we find the courage to create our most extraordinary lives."*
>
> —*Coach Charlene*

There is an African proverb: "If we stand tall, it is because we stand on the shoulders of many ancestors." As we look throughout history, we see phenomenal leaders, activists, and everyday individuals who were chosen to stand against injustice and racism, even at the cost of their own lives. This legacy is what compelled me to speak up. I could no longer remain silent. It was my moment to be innovative and transformative—the moment that chose me.

We stand on the courage and vision of pioneers like Rosa Parks, Martin Luther King Jr., Mother Teresa, and Nelson Mandela, who bravely challenged the injustices of their time. Innovators like Steve Jobs, Alexander Graham Bell, George Washington Carver, and Dr. Daniel Hale Williams also seized their moments, changing the world with their groundbreaking contributions.

I firmly believe each of us has had moments in our lives when we've been called to respond to a unique, destiny-filled opportunity created just for us. It may not always be about speaking up against injustice, but I guarantee it is about giving voice to something important the world needs. It could be speaking up when something doesn't align with your values or your organization's vision or perhaps stepping in to support a colleague who's being treated unfairly.

Maybe your moment involves a burning desire, a dream you've held onto, or an idea you know would improve your life or benefit those you are called to serve. It might be as significant as starting a business or as deeply personal as choosing to forgive the very system you work for—which, in turn, could bring you a profound sense of freedom.

There are destiny moments throughout our journey, provided we haven't turned a deaf ear to them. Deep within, there is a yearning—a whisper that stirs restlessness with our current state. This inner voice nudges us to a path we've avoided. Why do we avoid it? Because it forces us out of our comfort zone. It pushes us to confront unfamiliar territory, compelling us to learn something new or take actions we've never taken before. This avoidance is natural. We cling to what is safe and known, even if it no longer serves us.

But in life, we always have a choice. Each decision presents a pivotal choice point—either propelling us into the unknown to our destiny or keeping us trapped in the comfort of familiar circumstances. The path of growth is often uncomfortable and choosing it can feel daunting. Yet this very discomfort is where transformation happens. The decision we make in these moments can either embitter us, keeping us stagnant and fearful, or empower us to grow stronger, wiser, and more aligned with our true purpose.

Being imprisoned in current circumstances feels like being trapped in a cycle where comfort and routine overshadow our potential for growth and change. Fear of the unknown and reluctance to step beyond our comfort zones keep us tethered to situations that no longer fulfill us. This kind of self-imprisonment manifests through fear of change, the deceptive allure of routine, and societal pressures that reinforce staying within the familiar.

For many years I was deeply entrenched in a stable healthcare career. Tasks that once sparked excitement gradually became mundane, dulling my sense of purpose and passion. Despite a persistent yearning for something more, fear held me back from venturing into the unknown.

I realized, during a moment of profound restlessness, I was imprisoning myself in circumstances which no longer nurtured my personal and professional growth. The fear of leaving behind what I knew, of stepping into something unfamiliar, felt overwhelming. But I knew deep inside the comfort zone would only stagnate me further.

Breaking free required confronting those deep-seated fears, embracing the uncertainty, and trusting my discomfort was part of the path forward. I had to acknowledge the pivotal choice in front of me: stay stagnant or take the leap to my destiny. I chose to step into the discomfort. This journey involved reevaluating my priorities, seeking mentorship, and taking deliberate steps toward a career aligned with my passions and values. Through this process, I discovered while familiarity offers security, true fulfillment lies beyond the boundaries of comfort.

Every decision point presents an opportunity: either remain trapped in the safety of routine or embrace the transformational change discomfort offers. It can lead to bitterness through stagnation or it can foster resilience and growth through courageous action.

Have you ever had a moment change the trajectory of your life? I've had moments that called me into them, but I can't say I responded to each one. There are moments in life which beckon us to step into a deeper calling within ourselves. If we can push past the pain and uncertainty, we will not only hear what our heart is saying but also witness the fruit of responding to the moment. It is in this moment of clarity the path shifts, and our journey changes direction.

For me, it was time to be a voice for those who had chosen silence within the four walls of our institutions. Silence born out of fear. It was time for me to be okay with speaking my truth for the greater good. It wasn't that people weren't talking. In fact, there was plenty of chatter. But the conversations I witnessed were counterproductive, filled with empty words and no action. The time for such talk had passed.

I had spent my entire career within different organizations, silently witnessing injustice, unable to speak up. But this time, something shifted. I began to listen to the voices of others who had also been treated unjustly, and I realized this moment was different. I couldn't remain silent any longer. I had to seize the moment.

As I heard Dr. Ronald Copeland say in a 2020 speech, "There are times when we seize a moment, and there are times when the moment chooses us." This moment chose me, and I said yes to the call. I initiated conversations about racism and inequity and created spaces where healing and transformation could begin through personal stories. This was my moment, in the space where I was leading. Your moment may look different, but I promise you will recognize it when it arises.

There's a passage of Scripture that says, "You didn't choose me. I chose you. I appointed you to go and produce lasting fruit, so that the Father will give you whatever you ask for, using my name" (John 15:16 NLT). These destiny moments choose us because of the deep desires in our hearts to make a difference in the world. So, who am I speaking to today? Are you one of those who have stayed silent but now feel it's time to release your voice? How many moments have passed you by because of fear, uncertainty, or the lure of the comfort zone? There is someone out there waiting for you to respond to your destiny moment because you are the answer to their problem.

What's in a moment?

Every day grants us one thousand, four hundred and forty minutes. Precious, irreplaceable minutes. Surely you deserve to claim your share. According to the Merriam-Webster dictionary, a moment is an instant, a split second, a point in time, or a crucial juncture. Ralph Waldo Emerson once wisely noted every minute spent in anger robs us of sixty seconds of happiness. Think for a moment: a normal resting heart rate for adults ranges from sixty to one hundred beats per minute. So, when I indulge in anger, frustration, or any negative emotion for just one minute, I sacrifice sixty irreplaceable heartbeats—sixty moments of peace, joy, or productivity.

Negative emotions like anger are inevitable on life's journey. But we are not meant to take up residence there. The purpose of bringing this up is to invite you to take stock of how you are spending your heartbeats—your moments. Consider your age, your experiences. How have you invested those moments? Have you lived them fully, or have you let them slip through your fingers, caught in cycles of distraction or fear?

Moments are extraordinary because they are finite and irreversible. Once a moment passes, it is gone forever, beyond our grasp. We are only allotted a certain number of heartbeats in a lifetime. Each one is a gift, and it is critical to stay conscious of how we spend them—or invest them. Life isn't just a series of days or years. It is made up of individual moments. The quality of our lives is directly tied to how we choose to invest those moments.

Life unfolds moment by moment. Some moments are filled with joy and opportunity, while others test our resilience and resolve. But every moment matters. Every second holds the potential to shape the direction of our lives. As you prepare for each day, each experience, ask yourself: what have I been doing with the moments I've had? Do I invest them in things that align with my values, my passions, and my purpose? Or am I letting them slip by, unnoticed, unclaimed?

This entire journey we call life boils down to moments. They are the building blocks of our destiny. To change the trajectory of your life, you must first take an honest inventory of how you've been spending those moments. You cannot arrive at a destination if you are unaware of where you currently stand. Reflection is the key. Take stock of your moments. Invest them with intention. Make them count.

One more sobering thought: if your heart is still beating, then you have time to create moments that count.

A moment to release your past

Time is measured by the passing of years, but life is lived in the present moment. As you dive into these pages, seize this opportunity. Not just to read, but to reflect. Refine your purpose, reset your goals, and most importantly, bury the past. Let this be your moment to step boldly into a future full of possibility.

The powerful words of evangelist Claudette Copeland ring true: "Don't hold onto your history at the expense of your destiny." How often do we find ourselves bound to the past, unable to move forward, trapped in cycles of regret, guilt, or pain? The truth is, if you're holding onto your past, you are imprisoning yourself in the present. Don't get me wrong, we must learn from our history, so I am not talking about ignoring the rich lessons learned.

Whatever happened in your past—whether it was something done to you, a decision you regret, or opportunities that didn't unfold as expected—it belongs where it happened: in the past. The more you drag it into your present, the more it weighs you down, causing frustration, bitterness, and a paralyzing sense of hopelessness. It's like a rope tied around your waist, with your past constantly pulling you back, no matter how hard you try to move forward. You may have motion, but you will lack progress. You'll be busy, but stagnant.

I understand. I know there were unfair, undeserved moments in your past. But if you're reading these words, you're still here. Your heart is still beating, and there's still time to create something new, to write a new story, to turn a new page. Your past does not define you unless you allow it to. This very moment is your opportunity to break free.

As I said earlier, you cannot get *there* until you are fully present *here*. Face your past. Acknowledge it. Resolve what needs to be resolved, and then let it go. If the people or situations that hurt you are no longer part of your life, why are you still carrying them with you? Let go of what's dead and release the burden holding back your momentum. Don't waste another heartbeat dwelling on what could have been or should have been.

Escaping the grip of past failures is hard, but it's necessary for your growth. It's necessary for you to reclaim your power, to foster resilience, and to step into the fullness of your potential. You are not defined by what has happened to you; you are defined by what you do with this moment, right now.

Learn from your past, but don't let it eclipse your future. Break free from the chains of history and let your present moment be the foundation for a brighter tomorrow. If you did waste heartbeats before reading this, redemption has come. This is your moment. Right now.

What will you do with it?

Summary

Chapter 2, "A Moment to Embrace," explores the transformative power of stepping into uncertainty and seizing destiny moments. Coach Charlene reflects on her journey of courageously initiating critical conversations on racism and inequities, urging readers to recognize and respond to the moments that call them. This chapter highlights the synergy between vulnerability and courage, showing how they unlock opportunities for personal growth and innovation. With inspiring insights, it encourages readers to trust their inner voice, lean into support systems, and find strength amid life's unpredictability, transforming challenges into pathways for renewal and impact.

Key Takeaways

- » **Courage**: Growth requires stepping into the unknown with faith and determination.
- » **Vulnerability**: Embracing uncertainty opens doors to self-discovery and transformation.
- » **Strength in Community**: Surrounding ourselves with a supportive network enhances our ability to navigate uncertainty.

Reflective Questions

1. What uncertainties have you faced, and how did you find the courage to embrace them?
2. Who or what serves as a source of strength when you encounter challenges?
3. How can you foster a sense of courage within your team or community?

Reflective Questions

Reflective Questions

CHAPTER 3

A Moment to Awaken

Recognizing the Whispers

"Listen to the whispers of your soul and the subtle nudges of the spirit. The signs are not mere coincidences; they are the Creator leading you to your highest purpose."

—*Coach Charlene*

Pre-pandemic, I found myself in a state of frustration and restlessness. My soul stirred, my heart yearned, and my spirit nudged me. However, amid my relentless work, I failed to slow down and listen to the quiet voice within. Have you ever found yourself grinding through life, ignoring the gentle whispers of your heart trying to tell you something? In the relentless pace of pre-pandemic life, I often did. Frustration and restlessness simmered beneath the surface, despite outward appearances of resilience and determination. These feelings intensified as 2020 unfolded—a year marked by COVID-19, heightened racial injustices, and personal challenges that pushed us all into uncharted territory.

Exhaustion settled deep within, echoing through different parts of my life. Each new demand felt heavier, yet I continued to say yes to everyone else, neglecting my own needs. As a leader dedicated to nurturing others, I realized I had failed to extend the same compassion to myself. It was during a moment of vulnerability, sitting in a virtual healing circle, the truth hit me. The facilitators' gentle prompts led me to introspection, revealing a stark reality—I had consistently prioritized the needs of my organization and others over my own well-being.

This pattern of neglect had profound consequences. I found myself depleted, both physically and emotionally. The energy I poured into supporting the organization left me drained and unable to tap into my own creativity and passion. I began to feel a growing sense of resentment, not toward those I helped, but to myself for neglecting my own needs. This neglect didn't just affect my personal life. It deeply impacted my joy and satisfaction in my professional life.

As a leader I found myself going through the motions, leading but also losing the meaning and purpose that once fueled me. Even though outwardly I showed up smiling, positive, and impactful, something deep within my soul remained unfulfilled. As others would come to my office, I noticed many around me were just going through the motions, coming to work, performing their tasks, and going home without a sense of fulfillment. This façade of productivity can be deceiving. It's easy for high achievers to stay busy, avoiding the whispers of their hearts and the nudges of their souls.

To continue to lead effectively and authentically, I needed to rediscover my own sense of wellbeing, purpose, and fulfillment. I needed to start being true to myself. I came across an anonymous saying that resonated deeply: "You don't die when your heart stops beating, you die when your heartbeats have no meaning!" What a sobering realization. The meaning and purpose had drained away because of constantly being too busy to think and also prioritizing others over myself. This quote caused me to be more selective and intentional about investing my heartbeats wisely moving forward.

Recognizing the importance of self-compassion became a turning point. I acknowledged that, like everyone else, I am human—prone to mistakes, setbacks, and the need for grace. Embracing self-compassion meant treating myself with the same kindness and understanding I readily offered others. It meant learning to say no when necessary, and embracing moments of pause and reflection.

Loving oneself enough to prioritize personal well-being isn't just self-care rituals or acts of kindness, it is fundamental self-respect. It is honoring the whispers of our soul and the nudges of the Spirit which guide us to our true purpose. This journey to self-love and self-compassion is a profound act of liberation, allowing us to live authentically and with greater fulfillment.

Summary

Chapter 3, "A Moment to Awaken," invites readers into the profound journey of awakening to the whispers that subtly guide us to our life's true purpose. Coach Charlene shares her deeply personal experience of learning to listen to the inner stirrings of her soul—those quiet yet persistent nudges pointing her to a calling greater than herself. These whispers often come in moments of stillness or during life's most challenging times, serving as a compass toward alignment with one's deeper mission.

This chapter emphasizes the transformative power of self-awareness, urging readers to pay attention to persistent, recurring passions, ideas, or thoughts. It highlights how these whispers are not random; they are the voice of purpose trying to break through the noise of daily life. By creating intentional space for mindfulness and reflection, readers can begin to discern the paths they are uniquely meant to follow.

Coach Charlene challenges readers to embrace these moments of awakening as opportunities to align their lives with their highest potential. Whether it's pursuing a long-buried dream, stepping into a leadership role, or advocating for change, this chapter inspires a deeper connection to purpose. It serves as a call to action, reminding readers the whispers within are often the first step to transformative action and meaningful impact.

This chapter is a powerful reminder that recognizing and acting on the whispers isn't just a personal journey—it is a catalyst for change in the lives of others. By listening to the call of your inner voice, you unlock the courage and clarity needed to step into your destiny.

Key Takeaways

- » **Self-Awareness:** Recognizing the whispers of our heart reveals our true purpose.
- » **Alignment:** Our inner voice often points us to the work we are uniquely called to do.
- » **Mindfulness:** Paying attention to life's nudges helps us stay aligned with our greater mission.

Reflective Questions

1. What recurring thoughts or passions keep tugging at your heart?
2. How can you create space for stillness to hear the whispers of your inner voice?
3. In what ways are you being called to step into greater alignment with your purpose?

Reflective Questions

Reflective Questions

CHAPTER 4

A Moment to Overcome

Navigating Life's Challenges with Resilience

"Challenges are not roadblocks; they are steppingstones on the path to your greatness. With resilience and determination, you can overcome any obstacle and emerge stronger than ever before."
—*Coach Charlene*

A Moment to Love the Unlovable

Have you ever had moments where you had to love beyond yourself? I watched my parents demonstrate this continually as I was growing up, but I never imagined I would be tested in so many ways as I went through life. My story of having to practice this idea of loving beyond will be totally different from yours, but I guarantee you have had to practice it. Whether you practiced it and failed or triumphed, you've had moments where you had to forgive and let things go to find freedom. Or maybe you have not gotten to the place of forgiveness yet. Nevertheless, there is a place of healing waiting for you if only you would forgive. Let me share a story which has impacted my life forever.

Charlene's Story:
From Transformation to Transcendence

I was an exceptional student, consistently earning A's and B's throughout my academic journey. I disliked missing school so much, the only time I was absent was due to an emergency surgery to remove my appendix during high school, and recovery afterward—a traumatic experience, as it marked the first instance of my absence. I graduated eighth in my class, but the lack of resources and readily available support or scholarships left me without funds for further education.

I grew up in the mid-sixties in a divided town, with whites on one side and blacks on the other. I was the first in my family to pursue higher education—a fact I'm truly grateful for. My hardworking parents provided excellent family support, but there was no extra money for school.

With about a year left to graduate, I found myself pondering my life's direction while heading to the mall. Unsure of what to do next, despite my academic success, I stumbled upon a sign: "Army College Fund $25,000." The allure drew me in, and I found myself signing up for the U.S. Army's early entry program. Although I didn't fully understand what I was doing, it felt like the right move. As a matter of fact, it was one of the best moves of my life.

Fast forward, I graduated, joined the U.S. Army, underwent boot camp and training, and was eventually discharged to pursue my desire to become a nurse.

While in nursing school, I encountered a pivotal moment which tested my ability to love beyond myself. I was caring for an older white woman who hadn't seen her family in a while. My goal for the day was to dress her up and make her feel beautiful for their visit. However, this well-intentioned moment turned traumatic when, after introducing myself, commencing to clean her up, she grabbed my wrist, dug her sharp fingernails in, looked me in the eyes, and shouted—get your hands off me you n******. *Yes!* That is what she said! I was frozen in shock and not sure what to do or say, so I continued to clean her up. As a child I always heard there was a devil on one side of your ear and an angel on the other. Well, as I cleaned her up, a torrent of thoughts flooded my mind—a distinct voice arose (most likely the devil), "Just put a pillow over her head." Almost immediately, another thought countered, "What if she was your mother?" I heard a voice within urging me to love beyond. In a shocking moment, I pressed through the pain to achieve my goal, but the encounter lingered as a poignant memory of hate. This painful moment became an opportunity for me to drop from my head to my heart. I had a choice—to love beyond. I refused to let her hateful words define me. I chose to release love instead of hate. It was my decision, a choice to be better, not bitter. I have shared this story before with colleagues and many of them said—I don't know how you kept helping her, but that is the power of loving someone beyond. Love is the only force to allow you to transcend a moment such as this one.

While I didn't feel better in the moment, the experience empowered me over time. It showed me the depth of my capacity to love, a capacity instilled by my wonderful parents who not only demonstrated God's love but introduced me to it. As a child, my parents exemplified the principle of loving beyond, especially when I faced hurtful relationships outside the home. My father's servant heart, demonstrating love through actions, laid the foundation for the deep well of love guiding me in a challenging moment. It wasn't just words; it was a foundation of love. It continued to grow as I connected with a God who is love.

Choosing love despite having the right to hate was a testament to the values instilled in me from the beginning. In retrospect, I recognize this challenging scenario propelled me into the moment where I now use this story to help bring transformation to others. We must never underestimate the power of a story. What was sent to destroy and devalue me became the fuel that forced me to be the trailblazer and change-agent I am today.

I believe the way I handled this horrific experience played a major role in how I have led in the midst of all the challenges I have faced as a Black nurse and leader. There have been so many moments where I have had to love beyond in order to transform to transcend. I believe experiences, whether positive or negative, make us who we are and prepare us for our journey as we navigate through life.

Summary

This chapter illuminates the path of overcoming life's trials with unwavering resilience. Through her journey, Coach Charlene exemplifies how embracing personal struggles can lead to profound growth and transformation. She reflects on moments of adversity that tested her spirit but ultimately became steppingstones toward her purpose. This chapter empowers readers to see challenges not as roadblocks but as opportunities to cultivate strength, perseverance, and a renewed sense of direction.

It's an invitation to rise above obstacles and to harness the lessons learned from hardship as tools for empowerment and lasting change.

Key Takeaways

- » **Resilience:** Overcoming obstacles builds inner strength and fortifies our purpose.
- » **Perspective:** Challenges often reveal hidden strengths and clarify our vision.
- » **Adaptability**: Flexibility and resourcefulness are key to overcoming adversity.

Reflective Questions

1. What challenges have shaped your resilience and character?
2. How can you reframe obstacles as opportunities for growth?
3. In what ways can you support others who are navigating challenges of their own?

Reflective Questions

Reflective Questions

CHAPTER 5

A Moment to Align

Discovering Serendipity and Synchronicity

"In the dance of serendipity and synchronicity, miracles unfold, and destinies collide. Embrace the magic of unexpected encounters and the beauty of perfectly timed moments."

—*Coach Charlene*

Defining Moments

In this journey called life, there are inevitable moments—some that test and push us to our breaking point, leaving us uncertain of how to respond. Yet, within these moments of testing, there always exists a choice. A choice to be defined, disrupted, consumed, or confounded by the pain of the moment. Personally, I have made it a lifestyle to choose life over succumbing to the shadows of despair.

These defining moments possess the power to either propel us to our destiny or shackle us to the past. Too often, however, we find ourselves missing these pivotal moments. We are ensnared by distractions and life circumstances that sow confusion, frustration, and weariness. They leave us depleted of the energy needed to pursue our dreams or follow the deep desires of our hearts.

This book aspires to be a guide, urging you to recognize those moments calling you to dive deeper, reach further, or love more intensely.

My desire is to encourage you to lean into the critical crossroads that urge you to:

- » Embrace change
- » Disrupt the status quo
- » Extend forgiveness
- » Undergo transformation
- » Evolve into the highest expression of yourself

Welcome to your personal journey of awakening—your moment.

Life, with its ebb and flow, graces us with serendipities and synchronicities. Serendipities are the gifts not actively sought after, found in unexpected moments—even if they come cloaked in pain. Synchronicities are meaningful coincidences, like the moment I discovered Jean Watson's Theory of Caring Science just when I was at the point of burnout and searching for purpose. It was as if God had placed this theory in my path precisely when I needed it most, rekindling my passion for nursing leadership and guiding me toward my next chapter. These moments hint at a larger, interconnected pattern weaving through our lives, reminding us nothing is random and we are always being led toward our greater purpose. Throughout my journey as a nurse leader I have encountered many of these serendipities and synchronicities in my life.

Effecting Change Right Where You Stand

It is not the challenges we face but the potential within us that holds the power to create lasting change. No matter where you find yourself, you are equipped with the ability to make an impact. The key lies in recognizing and seizing the opportunity to effect change right where you stand.

Each of us is born with a unique contribution to offer the world, a purpose bringing fulfillment and joy. However, the whispers of the heart—those subtle tugs that guide us to our calling—often go unnoticed amid the chaos of daily life. It takes intention and awareness to hear them and courage to respond.

Let me share a profound moment in my journey which encapsulates this truth.

The Burnout That Led to Breakthrough

I began my nursing career in 1993, brimming with excitement and a deep sense of purpose. The work was rewarding, and I thrived on the difference I made in the lives of my patients. However, in 2007, I transitioned into leadership as an Assistant Nurse Manager (ANM), taking on the responsibility of caring for frontline staff in a greater capacity. While this new role initially fed my soul, the increasing demands and administrative tasks slowly pulled me away from the people I loved serving.

By 2009, I found myself at a breaking point. The constant grinding, long night shifts, and mounting busyness left me feeling drained. I was restless, unfulfilled, and burned out—yet I couldn't pinpoint why. I was simply going through the motions, unsure how to reignite the passion that had once driven me.

Then came a moment of serendipity. My organization introduced Dr. Jean Watson's Theory of Caring Science to its leadership team. As I sat in the session, a light switched on within me. The principles of Caring Science didn't just resonate—they awakened something profound. They reminded me of why I had entered this field and gave me language to express my deepest values.

Reinvigorated, I approached my Chief Nurse Officer with a sense of urgency, determined to become a Caritas Coach and a Certified HeartMath Trainer. These tools became the catalyst for reigniting my passion and enabling me to inspire others within the organization. In just a few short months, my journey took an extraordinary turn—one confirming my calling to bring light into institutional darkness, as Dr. Watson so eloquently describes. Little did I know, learning about Caring Science at this exact moment in my journey was not a coincidence—it was synchronicity at work. Just one month after being introduced to Jean Watson's theory, I found myself in a situation putting these principles to the test in the most profound way.

As we leave our homes for our places of employment, we never think twice about the impact we will make in someone's life or the impact on ours as we venture out to complete our usual daily routine. In 2010 I never imagined when I left my house this it would be the night I, along with many other caregivers, would be invited into a miracle.

A Night to Remember

When I arrived at work, the atmosphere was busy—you could feel it in the air. I decided to put on scrubs, just in case I was needed. Around 4 a.m., we heard the loudspeaker announce, "Code C, Labor and Delivery. Code C, Labor and Delivery." I swiftly went to the operating room to ensure the team had everything they needed, as this alert signified both a mother and baby were in trouble. We delivered a pale, frail baby who showed no signs of life—no heart rate, no breathing.

We anxiously worked, hoping for a flicker of life. Five minutes passed—no heart rate, no breathing. Ten minutes passed—still nothing. Fifteen minutes passed—nothing. Finally, after 17 intense minutes, the physician called the code and said, "Let's stop." Tears streamed down our cheeks. This couldn't be happening. We were supposed to help bring life, not death.

I was overcome with compassion, and I could feel the prayers in the room. I also felt compelled to act. Out of the blue, I felt the need to touch the little limp angel and silently speak life into him. I held his tiny, ice-cold hand and softly said, "God, grant this family a miracle tonight." I stepped aside and watched as the pediatrician reluctantly removed the breathing tube. The baby was wrapped and placed on the side of the warmer as the team continued the surgery on the mother. The atmosphere in the room was heavy with grief. It was so hard to continue. You could have heard a pin drop.

A Glimmer of Hope

Then, as we stood in disbelief, the pediatrician said, "I'm going to listen one more time." He leaned in, listened, and softly said, "Hey, there's a faint heart rate." I thought, *Oh my God!* I quickly grabbed the baby, zoomed to the SCN (Special Care Nursery), placed the baby on a warmer, and we began life-sustaining measures again. As I put him on the monitor, we saw a heart rate. Oh, the praise that erupted in the room! The celebration and rejoicing to follow were indescribable. This little lifeless angel declared he had a purpose bigger than life, and he wanted to fulfill it.

Doubt and Unbelief

In the days to follow, doubt tried to creep in. Questions arose: Would this baby ever wake up? Would he be able to eat, play, or live a normal life?

Some questioned why I even tried to resuscitate him again. All I could say was, "I believe in miracles." Three days later, we received an update: the baby was doing amazingly well—breathing on his own and looking good. He was sent home seven days after his birth. What a miraculous turnaround!

A Lasting Connection

A month later, our miracle team visited the baby's home. Tears, laughter, and joy filled the room as we held him close. Amazingly, the family lived just one minute from my new home. Coincidence? I think not. Over the years, we've maintained a wonderful connection with this family. They've invited us to significant events, including his baptism.

A Call to Be Present

This night was more than a miracle—it was a revelation. The moment transcended race, religion, and divisions. What remained was our shared humanity, bound by compassion, love, and an unyielding hope for life. It was a testament to the power of a Caring Moment—a moment that touched every soul in the room and left an imprint of light, love, and transformation. Jean Watson shares how the Caritas theory and principles are lived out in such caring moments.

As I reflect on this experience, I can't help but recall Jean Watson's profound words: "Maybe this one moment, with this one person, is the very reason we're here on Earth at this time." That night, I believe I was placed there for a purpose—to be an instrument of light, love, and hope. This miracle was a reminder. Sometimes, it is in the darkest of moments we find our greatest calling. This story is a testament to how you can effect change right where you are, by showing up, staying present, and embracing the profound moments life places before you.

I hope this story will ignite a flame inside of you that will cause you to go about your day recognizing you were born to touch lives, you were born to make a difference and to have an impact everywhere you go, even if it is just with a smile, a touch, or an embrace. However small it may seem to you, there is someone waiting for you to be a miracle in their lives.

I believe, with the theory of Caring Science as my foundation, and the ten caritas processes in my tool kit, I was able to infuse the practices, be sustained, and support those struggling mentally during the 2020 double pandemic.

The miracle moment was not just an isolated event but a pivotal experience that reshaped my understanding of the power of presence, compassion, and transformative action. It was the awakening that prepared me for what was to come—a season of unprecedented challenges testing the resilience and humanity of healthcare workers globally. As the world was thrown into chaos during the double pandemic of 2020—COVID-19 and systemic racism—I leaned heavily on the principles of Caring Science and HeartMath. This theory, rooted in love, empathy, and intentionality, became my anchor. It equipped me with the language and tools to navigate not only my own emotions but also to create an environment where others could find healing and connection amid the turmoil.

HeartMath became a critical part of my journey. It's not just about managing stress—it's about mastering your emotions and protecting your energy so you can show up as your best self, even in the hardest moments. Using simple, science-backed techniques, HeartMath helps regulate the nervous system, shifting from stress and overwhelm to balance and clarity. In those intense, emotionally charged moments of 2020, these practices gave me the ability to pause, reset, and respond with intention instead of being consumed by frustration or burnout. It taught me I had to cultivate inner coherence before I could hold space for others, aligning my heart, mind, and emotions so I could lead with compassion, resilience, and clarity.

With every breath, every pause, and every moment of self-regulation, I was able to step into the chaos as a force of stability. And that's exactly what so many around me needed—someone to not just acknowledge the pain but to foster an environment where healing and transformation could take root. HeartMath didn't just help me survive those moments; it empowered me to thrive through them and guide others to do the same

After experiencing such a profound transformation and finding language in Dr. Jean Watson's theory of Caring Science, I knew I had discovered something that could be readily applied as we cared for ourselves and others. The theory articulated how to *be* while *doing the work*. It all started with me rediscovering my why, and giving myself permission to love myself enough to listen and be led by the whispers of my heart.

Dr. Jean Watson's work reminds us that true healing begins with presence. When we show up for another person with an open heart—fully listening, without judgment—we create a sacred space for trust, understanding, and connection to flourish. It is in these moments, when we hold another's fears or tears without retreating, that we embody the essence of caring. This profound act of presence reaffirms our shared humanity and becomes a powerful force for transformation.

During the tumultuous events of 2020, this principle became a lifeline. Post-pandemic, as healthcare systems grappled with the emotional aftermath of the double pandemic, I found Watson's 10 Caritas Processes indispensable in providing language to preserve our humanity. Specifically, Caritas Process #5 says, "Allow for expression of positive and negative feelings-authentically listen to another person's story." This practice focused on cultivating forgiveness and accepting the full spectrum of emotions, and it resonated deeply in me.

Equipped with this language, I facilitated listening sessions during 2020, cultivating a refuge for open dialogue for staff to share their experiences, fears, and frustrations. These sessions, grounded in the principles of Caring Science, created a wave of healing and understanding. Over time, I expanded these sessions to include all who sought connection, affirming that in hearing one another, we sustain our collective humanity and move toward healing in meaningful ways.

The ability to truly hear someone's story and sit with them in their suffering is transformative—it creates a sacred places for healing and connection. What I discovered during this pivotal moment was that, right where I stood, I had the power to create meaningful change. By embracing the opportunity to lead listening sessions and nurture a safe environment for others, I was able to impact not only the individuals around me but also the entire organization. This wasn't just a fleeting effort. It created a profound ripple effect, leaving a lasting mark on the culture and humanity of the workplace.

This revelation—transformation is possible right where you are—is something I carry deeply. It's a testament to the fact we don't need to wait for a perfect moment or a new role to make an impact. You, too, can be a change agent or trailblazer, exactly where you are right now. You possess a wealth of gifts, skills, and talents uniquely yours. These qualities, shaped by your experiences and perspectives, equip you to contribute in ways no one else can. Your presence in this moment isn't accidental. It is purposeful. Trust that what is within you is enough to spark the change your environment needs.

It is no coincidence you are where you are. You are positioned here, at this moment, for a reason. Whether or not it feels significant to you right now, there's a purpose behind your presence in this space. You carry something within you—a set of gifts and insights—meant to be used right here, right now. Your specific combination of experiences, whether they be professional, personal, or even spiritual, has uniquely equipped you to affect change in this environment.

You may not realize it yet, but you have the power to influence change. Your ideas, your voice, and your presence hold immense value. Whether you're the quiet observer who notices the details others miss, or the visionary who dreams of new possibilities, something about you can shift the atmosphere and inspire others. You might be the compassionate listener who fosters an environment for people to feel heard, or the strategic thinker who knows how to solve complex problems. Perhaps you are the motivator, the person who brings out the best in others and empowers them to pursue their goals.

Every one of us carries something extraordinary, something irreplaceable. Your specific combination of skills—whether it's leadership, creativity, empathy, resilience, or wisdom—gives you the ability to affect change in a way only you can. You are in your current position not by accident, but because there's something in this moment only you can do. You have what it takes to challenge the status quo, to ignite a spark of innovation, or to be the voice of justice and compassion in your sphere of influence.

Remember, change doesn't always start with grand gestures—it begins in the small, seemingly insignificant moments where we choose to step forward and speak up, to offer a solution, or to bring a fresh perspective. Each action you take, no matter how small, can ripple, creating a larger wave of transformation.

Don't wait for permission, and don't underestimate the impact you can have. You are here for a reason, and you are more equipped than you know. Your journey, your story, and your abilities are the perfect tools to implement change right where you are. The world needs what only you can offer. Step into your role as a change agent today—right here, right now. Here are a few gems to inspire you to impact your world, right where you stand.

Taking Action: Steps to Effect Change

Survey your surroundings—what can you do in your immediate sphere to become a catalyst for change? Remember, this isn't about transforming the entire world all at once. It is discerning what lies within your sphere of influence and making a meaningful difference there. Often, transformative moments choose us, presenting a profound opportunity to create impact. To seize these moments, consider these four essential steps:

1. Identify and Embrace the Tug

The first step in becoming a change agent is to recognize the subtle tugs at your heart and soul. These tugs are the whispers of your inner self, pointing you toward what truly matters. What thoughts keep resurfacing in your mind? What issues ignite a fire within you? Pay close attention to which topics dominate your conversations, which causes stir your deepest passions, and which concerns keep you awake at night. These are often the indicators of where your purpose lies.

For me, this tug became undeniable during one of the most challenging seasons of my life. I went to prayer seeking clarity, and the words I heard pierced through every doubt: *What you do in this moment will determine your destiny and dictate your future.* This whisper wasn't just a gentle nudge—it became a roar that shook me to my core, compelling me to take action. It was a soul-deep pull I could no longer ignore.

Embracing the tug means acknowledging these feelings instead of pushing them aside. These inner pulls are a call to action—an invitation to step into your moment. It's easy to wait for someone else to lead, but true change begins when you decide to take the first step. Don't hesitate. When you feel that nudge, trust it is a signal guiding you toward the change you were meant to create. Just as I found the courage to act on that whisper, so can you. In these moments of alignment with your purpose, you will discover the strength to move forward, knowing you are being called to something greater than yourself.

2. Study and Master the Topic

Once the tug of purpose became undeniable, I knew I couldn't move forward without equipping myself with knowledge—or so I thought. The truth was, I already had the knowledge within me. Years of experience, countless observations, and a deep understanding of the issues I felt called to address were all there, waiting to be unleashed. What I needed wasn't more knowledge—it was the courage to speak up and let the knowledge flow out of me.

I began by revisiting the insights I had gathered over the years, diving into statistics, conducting interviews, and immersing myself in the stories of those around me. These actions didn't just deepen my understanding.

They reinforced the truth I had long known but hesitated to voice. Passion alone wasn't enough—I had to marry it with the wisdom I already possessed and the confidence to share it boldly.

Mastering the topic, for me, wasn't about acquiring something new but about trusting the knowledge already within me and refining it through intentional learning. This process became transformative. Each time I leaned into my expertise and allowed it to flow, I felt more empowered and equipped to address the challenges before me. The more I embraced my voice and experience, the more credibility and confidence I gained, enabling me to create meaningful change.

3. Move

When the moment chooses you, hesitation is not an option. For me, the calling to act during the racial unrest of 2020 was not a gentle nudge. It was a commissioning—a demand for action I could not ignore. The words I heard during prayer, *What you do in this moment will determine your destiny and dictate your future,* were so powerful they left no room for doubt. Even if I had wanted to retreat, the force of the calling propelled me forward.

As someone who had navigated the ranks as a Black woman in healthcare leadership, I was no stranger to discomfort. I had spent years being uncomfortable—challenged by microaggressions, systemic inequities, and spaces where I was often the only one who looked like me. So when the moment chose me, I was ready to respond not because it was easy, but because my life had already prepared me for it. Discomfort was familiar. Inaction was not an option.

This was not about waiting for perfect conditions or finding the courage to act—it was about responding to a calling so strong it demanded immediate action. I knew my voice, my experience, and my presence were needed in this moment, no matter the potential backlash or challenges. Speaking up felt less like a choice and more like a necessity, a responsibility to those who came before me and those who would come after.

When you feel the call to move, trust it. Often, we are already equipped with what we need. We just have to lean into the moment and allow the action to flow. The call itself is your confirmation—it tells you you are ready, even if it doesn't feel like it at the time. Move boldly, knowing your voice and your actions have the power to create ripples of change which extend far beyond the immediate moment.

4. Stay True to Your Assignment

Motivational speaker Lisa Nichols once said, "Convenience and conviction cannot live on the same block." These words resonated deeply with me because staying true to your assignment often means choosing conviction over convenience. It means showing up and using your voice, even when it's uncomfortable, inconvenient, or requires sacrifices.

When the moment chose me, the path was anything but easy. There were times when staying silent would have been far more convenient, when shrinking back into the shadows would have felt safer. But conviction wouldn't allow it. The weight of my calling compelled me to speak up, to act, and to lead—even when it required me to step into difficult conversations, address systemic issues, and challenge the status quo.

Staying true to your assignment isn't just about resilience—but about alignment. It's ensuring every action you take reflects your values, your purpose, and the unique gifts you bring to the table. For me, this meant consistently using my voice to create safe spaces, inspire change, and uplift those who felt unseen or unheard. It meant holding onto my mission, even when the journey felt lonely and isolating.

Because here's the truth: sometimes staying true to your assignment places you on a solitary path. The decisions you make may not be understood by everyone, and the actions you take might not garner instant validation. But this is where trust in the process becomes essential. You have to believe your conviction is leading you in the right direction, even when the road feels uncertain or the support feels scarce.

This unwavering commitment creates a ripple effect. When you stay true to your assignment, you not only honor your own calling, but you also inspire others to step into their purpose. Your conviction becomes contagious, empowering others to find their voices and make their own impact.

Remember, the road to fulfilling your assignment will not always be smooth, but it will always be worth it. Conviction demands courage, and staying true to your purpose ensures the legacy you leave behind is one of transformation, authenticity, and unwavering impact. Let your actions be a testament to your commitment to make a difference—no matter how challenging or lonely the path may become. Trust the process, because the journey is shaping you for something greater than you can imagine.

The journey to becoming a change agent begins with embracing the tug, equipping yourself with knowledge, stepping into bold action, and staying true to your mission. The path is rarely straight, often challenging, and sometimes lonely. Yet, every step—every sacrifice, every lesson—is undeniably worth it.

If you're feeling the stirrings of a moment calling you to act, it's not by accident. That pull on your heart is a sign the world needs what only you can bring. Your unique combination of experiences, skills, and passion is not just valuable—it's essential. You are here for a reason, and your voice has the power to shape the future.

Don't wait for perfect conditions or a roadmap to appear. The tug is your signal, and the courage to take the first step is the only permission you need. Trust that even the smallest action can create ripples of change. Whether you start by having one difficult conversation, designing a new initiative, or taking a leap into the unknown, your contribution has the potential to inspire and transform.

The world is waiting—not for someone else, but for you. Your moment has chosen you, and within it lies the power to ignite change, touch lives, and leave a legacy. Step into the call with conviction, knowing your courage will light the way for others.

This is your moment. Will you rise to it? Will you answer the call and become the change agent the world so desperately needs? The time is now, and the choice is yours. Step boldly into your destiny and let your journey inspire others to do the same.

Summary

In Chapter 5, "A Moment to Align," Coach Charlene reflects on how life's serendipitous and synchronous moments revealed the interconnectedness of her journey and purpose. She illustrates how aligning with her inner calling allowed her to recognize opportunities disguised as challenges, ultimately leading to miraculous transformations both personally and professionally. This chapter inspires readers to trust in the timing of their lives, embrace the beauty of unforeseen alignments, and understand every moment has the potential to steer them toward their destiny. It's a reminder nothing is random—everything has purpose when viewed through the lens of alignment and faith.

Key Takeaways

- » **Serendipity**: Unexpected moments often guide us toward our greater purpose.
- » **Synchronicity:** Meaningful coincidences reveal the interconnectedness of our journeys.
- » **Alignment:** When purpose and opportunity align, miracles and transformation follow.

Reflective Questions

1. How has serendipity played a role in shaping your path?
2. What moments of synchronicity have affirmed your purpose?
3. How can you stay open to opportunities that align with your values?

Reflective Questions

Reflective Questions

CHAPTER 6

A Moment to Transform

Embracing Personal Growth and Change

"Transformation is not a destination but a journey of self-discovery and growth. Embrace the process, trust the journey, and allow yourself to bloom into the fullest expression of who you are meant to be."
—*Coach Charlene*

How do you personally respond to extreme setbacks? It is natural to initially react, but the power lies in shifting your reaction into a measured response. Mastering this art can save us immeasurable heartache and pain. The traumatic experiences we all endure have the potential to:

- » make us bitter or better
- » open us up or shut us down
- » give us opportunity to forgive or imprison us in resentment
- » cause us to jump into action or stay rooted in fear
- » make us grow or remain complacent
- » allow us to be remembered or forgotten

True power lies in what you choose to do at that moment. That choice is what will define you.

Dr. Al Siebert, author of *The Resiliency Advantage*, discusses how people react to life's blows in various ways. Some of us explode emotionally.

Others implode: turn inward and become numb. Some develop a victim's mentality, while others demonstrate remarkable resilience, adapting quickly to adverse circumstances and thriving. Recognize life will have its share of ups and downs. So, we must commit to becoming better human beings by doing what is within our control to cultivate healthier and more fulfilling lives.

I would never have been able to handle any of the moments I shared with you in the previous chapter if I had not been working on myself throughout my life. Actress and activist Sophia Bush once said, "You are allowed to be both a masterpiece and a work in progress simultaneously." This quote is a profound reminder of the duality of our human experience—the constant interplay between our growth and our inherent worth. Too often, we are quick to judge ourselves harshly when we fall short, forgetting mistakes and setbacks are integral to the process of becoming.

There will be moments when we feel on top of the world, and moments when we stumble and fall, questioning our worth and abilities. Yet even in our lowest points, the masterpiece within us remains intact, waiting to be rediscovered and refined. This truth is the foundation of resilience—the ability to embrace imperfection, extend grace to ourselves, and keep moving forward. Holding onto the belief that we are both a masterpiece and a work in progress allows us to navigate challenges with courage and hope, knowing every misstep is an opportunity for growth and transformation.

I have shared my moment—the moment that chose me—and how it became a catalyst for finding my voice, sharing my story, and driving change amid the racial unrest and the profound challenges of 2020 and beyond. But now, let me turn the table to you and your moment.

Moments of reckoning come for all of us—those pivotal junctures which demand a response, a shift, and sometimes a leap of faith. My question to you is this: When your moment chose you, how did you respond? Did it move you into action or leave you standing still? Did you step forward into the discomfort of growth, or did you shrink back into the familiarity of silence?

How has the moment shaped who you are today? Were you compelled to rise, to change, to contribute in ways you hadn't before? Or did fear and uncertainty hold you captive, leaving the moment unanswered? Did you take time to examine yourself—your values, your intentions, your purpose? Or did the noise of life drown out the whisper calling you to transform?

These questions are not meant to accuse or condemn, but to invite reflection. They are a call to pause, to look within, and to ask yourself: Who am I now because of that moment? What have I learned? What am I still holding back? Your moments—whether you recognized them at the time or not—hold immense power. They are opportunities to rewrite your story, to disrupt what no longer serves you, and to create a ripple effect of change. The question is, will you answer the call?

That moment, the double pandemic, chose us all. It presented a profound opportunity to pause, reflect, and ensure that we allowed the moment to inform, transform, and disrupt not only ourselves but also our families, schools, hospitals, communities, judicial systems, states, nation, and world.

To those of you who launched out into the deep waters, who said, "I don't know what to do, but I am open to learning. I don't know what to say; I don't want to say the wrong thing. I am hurt, but I rise. I am wounded, but I still believe"—I applaud you. I want to say, "Thank you! Thank you for having the courage to stare injustice in the face and choose not to accept the status quo any longer. Thank you for sharing your truth unapologetically. Thank you for being a part of the change by being okay with not being okay at times!"

I encourage you to slow down, get quiet, and assess your current state. As we continue to navigate these tumultuous waves called life, remember you have been chosen for this moment. Every moment presents a choice to:

» react or respond
» speak up or stay silent
» support or ignore
» retreat or advance
» seek knowledge or remain ignorant
» love or hate
» forgive or stay imprisoned

We always have a choice! I am more resilient than ever now because I took care of my spirit, soul, and body through the pandemic. We have endured so much, but we can still choose to let what we've walked through make us bitter or better. Let's accept this transformative moment and emerge more powerful, more conscious, and more intentional—because we truly are better together.

Summary

Chapter 6, "A Moment to Transform," is a powerful exploration of the transformative process that unfolds when we embrace change with an open heart and mind. Coach Charlene shares her evolution from a place of burnout and disconnection to one of renewal and clarity through the integration of Caring Science principles. This chapter encourages readers to see personal growth not as a destination but as an ongoing journey of self-discovery and reinvention. By addressing their own vulnerabilities and stepping into their authentic power, readers are empowered to transform themselves and the systems they serve.

Key Takeaways

- » **Growth Through Reflection:** Transformation begins with introspection and the willingness to confront our own limitations.
- » **The Power of Change:** Embracing change creates opportunities for personal and professional evolution.
- » **Self-Love:** Prioritizing self-care and self-love allows us to show up as our best self for others.

Reflective Questions

1. What areas of your life or career are calling for transformation?
2. How can self-reflection help you identify and address areas for growth?
3. What steps can you take to practice self-love and care in your journey?

Reflective Questions

Reflective Questions

CHAPTER 7

A Moment to Prepare

*Being Ready When
Your Moment Chooses You!*

*"Prepare yourself not for the expected, but for the unexpected.
For when your moment chooses you, it is not a test of your readiness
but a testament to your resilience and inner strength."*
—Coach Charlene

Are you prepared for the moment?

How could I have been prepared for such a moment? The Merriam-Webster dictionary defines *prepared* as being ready beforehand for some purpose, use, or activity. It also means to be in a proper state of mind. I firmly believe each story and every experience I shared in this book and encountered in my life has prepared me for the next challenge or opportunity. The question I pose to you is this: Are you preparing for your moment? Even if you're unsure what the moment might be, the responsibility to prepare yourself remains. You must work diligently to become the highest expression of yourself, for you are your greatest asset.

As you read earlier in the book when I chose love, these moments, when they arrive, can be sobering. They will test every facet of your being.

That's why it's essential to invest in yourself now to build the resilience, wisdom, and emotional fortitude necessary to navigate life's inevitable challenges. The way you deal with upsets and adverse circumstances determines whether you will be ready when the moment chooses you.

When such a moment arrives, it's an opportunity to reveal whether you will react or respond. Reacting is often an automatic, emotional reflex—one which happens without conscious thought, often leading to anger, frustration, irritation, or fear. On the other hand, responding is a choice, a deliberate action guided by mindfulness and reflection. In *response* you find the power to shape the outcome of your destiny-defining moments.

Let me warn you, preparation is not a passive act but an active, ongoing process: sharpening your mind, nurturing your spirit, and cultivating the wisdom to discern how to act when life presents you with a critical choice. When a significant or destiny-defining moment unexpectedly presents itself, you won't have the luxury of time to get ready. You must *be* ready.

Although some moments in life will catch you off guard, and despite all the preparation in the world, you may still find yourself unprepared. There are steps you can take to increase your readiness. These steps are about taking responsibility for your growth, your decisions, and ultimately, your impact on the world. Let me share a few gems to help you prepare as much as you can, so when your moment comes, you can seize it with confidence, grace, and purpose.

Self-Discovery: Uncovering Your True Self

Embarking on a journey of self-discovery begins with the process of deep self-reflection. This exploration takes you into the very core of your being, prompting you to ponder your values, principles, and long-term aspirations. By intimately understanding what matters to you, you lay a solid foundation for navigating destiny moments with clarity and purpose. Along this introspective journey, it becomes imperative to identify your passions—those innate drives that fuel your soul and align with your strengths. These passions often serve as guiding stars, illuminating the path toward moments of destiny.

I recognized nursing was my occupation. It was my platform which was used to share my gifts. Beyond nursing as a career, my true vocation—my calling—was to inspire others to become better human beings. I came to understand I was more than a nurse. I was a servant of transformation, someone who could lead others to discover their own potential and purpose. This realization didn't come easily. It required peeling back layers of expectations placed upon me by others and rejecting lies that I wasn't enough or my dreams were too big.

The journey of self-discovery is not for the faint of heart. It is challenging, and many people never find their real selves because they are buried under the weight of others' expectations. Too often, we listen to the voices of others—sometimes even those we trust—and allow their truths to become ours. But what I've learned is you have to start by asking yourself the hard questions: Who am I, really? Why am I here? What do I really want? These aren't easy questions to answer, and they require you to dig deep, beyond the surface-level identities you've adopted.

Let's talk about the real you first. Out of the 8.2 billion people on earth, no one else has your fingerprint. Think about that. You are unique. You have no equal. You are incomparable. You are one of a kind—a designer's original. When God saw you, He equipped you with gifts, talents, and skills unique to you! There is no one else who has your smile, your voice, or your essence. Understanding this is where the journey of self-discovery truly begins.

The premise of becoming a better you is rooted in knowing who you are. You shed the masks you've worn to fit in, breaking free from the comfort zones that have kept you stagnant, and silencing the negative voices that have told you you're not enough. The real you is powerful beyond measure, crafted with a distinct purpose.

Yet, amid the pursuit of self-awareness, it's essential to avoid the pitfalls of overthinking. While preparation is undeniably crucial, excessive rumination can cloud your judgment and hinder your ability to trust your instincts when the moment beckons. Central to this journey is cultivating unwavering self-confidence—a belief in your inherent worth and capacity to make sound decisions for your own life. This self-assurance serves as a steadfast anchor, empowering you to navigate life's twists and turns with grace and conviction.

In the midst of uncertainty, trusting your spirit becomes invaluable. This innate intuition often offers profound insights and guidance, even in the most unexpected circumstances. By embracing your intuition, you reaffirm your trust in your own significance—a belief that propels you forward on your journey of self-discovery and personal growth.

As you embark on this profound exploration of self, may you uncover the depths of your being and emerge with a renewed sense of purpose and direction. This is not just about finding out what you're good at, but about discovering who you were created to be. When you know yourself—your calling, your purpose, your value—you become unstoppable. Your heart's whispers are there to guide you, leading you to a life which is not only fulfilling but also impactful. So, take the time to listen, to reflect, and to become the person you were always meant to be.

Lifelong Learner: Embracing Growth and Transformation

Once you discover who you are, the next crucial step is to decide to fully become that person. It's not enough to simply know your potential—you must actively choose to live it out every day. This decision requires a commitment to learning, unlearning, growing, and evolving continuously. Just as I did when I realized my purpose was not only nursing at the bedside, but in caring for the caregiver, I threw myself into learning about Caring Science, HeartMath, and other transformative practices. This journey of self-discovery and mastery empowered me to make a profound impact right where I was.

If we think we know it all, we have closed the door to learning, growth, and true wisdom. The moment we believe we have nothing left to learn is the moment we know nothing at all. Embracing the philosophy of a lifelong learner means embarking on a perpetual journey of growth and development. At its core lies a commitment to continuously hone and expand one's skills and knowledge base. This dedication to self-improvement is the cornerstone of navigating life's myriad challenges with confidence and agility. You recognize being well-prepared often requires a solid foundation of expertise—a commitment to mastering your craft and staying abreast of industry advancements.

Central to the spirit of a lifelong learner is the imperative to stay informed, to remain attuned to current events and trends within your field or area of interest. In a rapidly evolving world, knowledge is power, and staying informed equips you with the insights needed to respond effectively to changing circumstances. Whether it's through avid reading, attending workshops, or engaging in continuous education, staying informed fosters adaptability and resilience in the face of uncertainty.

But it's not just about acquiring knowledge for knowledge's sake. It's applying what you learn in meaningful ways. It's understanding that every piece of information you gather is a tool which can help you craft a better version of yourself and a better world for those around you. That's why I committed myself to mastering Caring Science and HeartMath principles along with the content I was creating. Not just to enhance my own skills, but to create environments where others could thrive as well.

Crucially, the lifelong learner remains steadfastly open-minded, embracing change as an inherent aspect of growth. Destiny moments often herald significant shifts in life's trajectory, presenting new opportunities and challenges alike. By cultivating a mindset of openness to change, you position yourself to embrace these pivotal moments with courage and grace. Stay receptive to new possibilities, even when they diverge from the familiar, and align them with your core values and aspirations. In essence, the lifelong learner approaches life as a perpetual journey of discovery, fueled by a relentless pursuit of knowledge, an unwavering openness to change, and a steadfast commitment to personal growth and fulfillment.

Becoming a lifelong learner means embracing the mindset that growth never ends. It's understanding every day is an opportunity to learn something new, to expand your understanding, and to apply what you've learned in ways that make a difference. It's being humble enough to recognize no matter how much you know, there is always more to learn. This mindset is what keeps you evolving, adapting, and ultimately, thriving in a world which is constantly changing.

In your own journey, ask yourself: Are you willing to become the person you were meant to be? Are you committed to learning, growing, and embracing the challenges that come your way? Are you willing to surrender those habits and behaviors that no longer serve you? Because in the end, the important thing is what you do with knowledge, and how you use it to make an impact on the world around you.

Build a Supportive Network and Take Action

Building a supportive network is paramount. No one achieves greatness alone. It's essential to connect with mentors who can offer valuable guidance and perspective during critical decision-making moments. These mentors, with their wisdom and experience, help you navigate the complexities of your path and provide the encouragement needed to keep moving forward. Cultivate meaningful relationships with friends, colleagues, and contacts, nurturing a strong network to provide both emotional support and opportunities for growth.

However, merely building connections isn't enough. Action is key. It's in the doing that dreams are realized. Seize opportunities as they arise, for hesitating can result in missed chances for growth and fulfillment. In my own journey, once I found my voice, I noticed others began to be drawn toward my message and my story. I started connecting with those who wanted to support, uplift, and be thought partners on this journey. As I embraced my authentic self and stepped into my purpose, the right people—those who were meant to be part of my destiny—were naturally drawn to me. This is the power of living in alignment with your true self.

When you find your voice and take action, the universe responds. Those who resonate with your purpose, who share your vision, and who can help you elevate your impact will be attracted to your light. It's a beautiful cycle: the more you step into your true self, the more you attract the people who will help you grow and succeed. This is why taking action is so crucial. And not just moving forward, but moving forward with the right people by your side.

Stay adaptable in the face of uncertainty, remaining flexible and willing to adjust plans to make the most of each moment. Life is unpredictable, and your ability to pivot when necessary will determine your success. Define your goals clearly, both short-term and long-term, ensuring your actions align with your aspirations. Prioritize effectively, determining what matters to you and allocating your time and energy accordingly.

In combining the strength of a supportive network with decisive action, you pave the way for a journey filled with purpose, growth, and achievement. When you take your first step, you begin to build momentum, and as you continue, you will find the right doors begin to open. The right people will show up, and the opportunities which align with your purpose will present themselves. This is how you create a life of significance—by recognizing you are never really alone, and by understanding that your actions, supported by the right network, can lead to extraordinary outcomes.

Take that step. Connect with those who inspire you, who challenge you, and who lift you up. Then, move boldly in the direction of your dreams, knowing you are supported and your actions have the power to change not just your life, but the lives of those around you.

A MOMENT TO PREPARE

Develop Resilience

Resilience has surely been my superpower throughout my journey. The power of building your resilience muscles cannot be understated. It is the foundation upon which all other strengths are built. My faith in God was paramount in navigating the myriad challenges I faced with grace and love. This unwavering faith served as my bedrock, providing the support and strength needed to move through each trial with purpose and poise.

Along my professional journey, becoming a HeartMath certified trainer was a game changer. It provided me with tools to intelligently manage my energy amid the chaos that often surrounds working in the healthcare system. These tools, combined with my faith, helped me stay grounded and resilient, even in the most tumultuous of times.

In the pursuit of navigating destiny moments, cultivating resilience becomes paramount. Resilience isn't only bouncing back from setbacks. It's embracing challenges as inherent components of growth. It is recognizing every difficulty is an opportunity to fortify yourself with adaptability and perseverance. Setbacks, while often inevitable, are not meant to derail you—they are opportunities for profound learning and personal development. These challenges serve as catalysts for growth, rather than deterrents to progress.

To maintain equilibrium amid life's upheavals, it is essential to stay grounded and effectively manage stress. Developing stress management techniques ensures that you maintain your composure in high-pressure situations, allowing for clear-headed decision-making and focused action. Mindfulness practices, such as meditation and prayer, serve as anchors, fostering a sense of centeredness and clarity amid life's tumultuous waves. These practices are not just about finding peace. They are about cultivating the inner strength needed to navigate through life's storms with grace.

A crucial aspect of resilience-building lies in honing the skill of decision-making. By making informed choices rooted in available information and personal values, individuals cultivate decisiveness—a trait invaluable when confronted with pivotal moments. Resilience also means mentally simulating various scenarios to prepare for different outcomes. This mental preparedness allows you to anticipate and navigate diverse situations with poise and confidence, no matter how unpredictable they may be.

Destiny moments are unpredictable and unique to each individual. By fostering spiritual, mental, emotional, and professional preparedness, you enhance your readiness to seize these moments and shape your future in alignment with your deepest goals and values. Through resilience, mindfulness, and informed decision-making, you embrace the transformative power of destiny moments, forging a path of purpose and fulfillment.

Resilience is not just a trait, it is a way of life. It's the ability to face challenges head-on, with the knowledge that you are equipped to handle whatever comes your way. Resilience is about standing firm in your beliefs, trusting in your inner strength, and moving forward with confidence, no matter the obstacles. When you cultivate resilience, you are not just preparing for the inevitable challenges—you are preparing to rise above them, to thrive in spite of them, and to emerge stronger on the other side.

Steps to respond to your moment

Life presents us with pivotal moments—those unexpected, often daunting instances with the potential to alter the course of our destiny. These moments rarely announce themselves with clarity. Instead, they arrive unbidden, woven into the fabric of our everyday lives, often disguised as challenges, disruptions, or even quiet nudges from within. The secret to navigating these defining moments lies in preparation—not just external readiness but an inner, intentional approach to self-awareness, resilience, and growth. Being prepared when your moment chooses you means stepping beyond the hypnotic rhythm of daily living, recognizing the significance of the moment, and allowing it to shape you into the fullest expression of your potential.

Step 1: Recognize the Moment

Many of us move through life on autopilot, lulled by the routine and the false sense of security offered by our comfort zones. In this state, we often fail to see the moments designed to wake us, to call us to something greater. These moments—sometimes subtle, sometimes jarring—are divine nudges, the Creator's way of shaking us awake and propelling us toward our purpose. Recognizing them requires more than just open eyes. It demands an awakened spirit and a readiness to see beyond the surface of the ordinary.

Too often, we let these transformative moments slip through our fingers because we mistake them for routine or allow fear to tether us to what is familiar. Life-changing moments don't wait for our permission or our readiness. They crash into our lives, demanding we take notice and act with courage. My journey toward leadership during the racial unrest of 2020 was born of such a moment. When the world seemed to crumble under the weight of injustice and uncertainty, I felt an undeniable pull—a call to step beyond my comfort zone and lead in ways I had never envisioned.

While many around me were understandably paralyzed by anger, grief, and trauma, I knew this moment had been stirring within me for years, preparing me for such a time as this. It was not a time to remain in the shadows but to step boldly into the light, driven by purpose and a cause far greater than myself.

To recognize such moments, we must intentionally sharpen our awareness and align with our inner truth. This begins with a commitment to mindfulness—pausing amid the busyness of life to see and feel what is unfolding around you. Embrace challenges as divine opportunities rather than obstacles, understanding discomfort often signals the start of transformation. Trust your intuition, the inner whisper that speaks before logic takes over. It is often your soul's way of guiding you toward something greater. Reflect on your core values, as they act as an internal compass, pointing you toward moments that align with your higher purpose. Journaling is a powerful tool for self-reflection, as it allows you to capture and revisit your experiences, uncovering patterns that might otherwise go unnoticed. Engaging in practices like meditation or quiet solitude can help attune your spirit to the subtle shifts in your life, enabling you to recognize moments of significance when they arise.

And please don't forget, you cannot do this alone. Surround yourself with people who inspire you and challenge you to be your best. Often, these relationships can serve as mirrors reflecting back the moments you might otherwise miss. Recognizing your moment requires an open heart, a discerning mind, and the courage to embrace the unfamiliar, knowing the path to your potential is paved with the stepping stones of awareness and intentional action.

Step 2: Respond to the Moment

When a pivotal moment arises, the way we respond holds the potential to drive us forward, inspire us to act, or stop us in our tracks. The instinctive reaction to unexpected situations is often emotional—a surge of fear, anger, or confusion clouds our judgment. While these initial feelings are valid and natural, the power lies in shifting from reaction to a thoughtful, intentional response. This shift requires self-awareness and a willingness to pause, reflect, and channel energy constructively.

One of the most profound lessons I learned as a leader is the importance of intelligently managing my energy. In 2012, I became a HeartMath Certified Trainer. HeartMath tools taught me the value of coherence—the alignment of the heart, mind, and emotions—and the transformative power of pausing before making a decision or delivering a response. In moments of high tension or uncertainty, I discovered simply taking a moment to breathe and reset could create the mental clarity needed to respond rather than react. This practice helped me maintain composure and effectiveness, even in the most challenging circumstances.

When the moment chose me during the racial unrest of 2020, I stood at a crossroads. My initial reaction was anger—an entirely human response to injustice and pain. Yet, what I chose to do after the first wave of emotion was the real turning point. Instead of being consumed by frustration, I paused, centered myself, and reflected on how I could use this moment to lead with purpose. That pause, that breath, became the bridge between reaction and response, allowing me to anchor my actions in my values and make a meaningful impact.

Responding to a moment requires stepping out of your comfort zone. Growth rarely occurs in the safety of familiarity. It is found in challenges that stretch us, disrupt our routines, and compel us to expand our capabilities. This step also demands conviction and adaptability. When you are clear about your values and flexible in your approach, you can navigate even the most unpredictable situations with confidence and grace.

But responding is not just about personal growth, it has to do with the influence you have on others. A thoughtful response can inspire those around you to act with intention and purpose. Each time I chose to respond to life's challenges with measured and deliberate action, I found opportunities not only to grow as a leader but also to create ripples of transformation in those I served.

HeartMath's tools of coherence and energy management have become foundational in my life and leadership. Pausing to breathe and recalibrate before speaking or deciding is not just a tool, it's a practice of empowerment. When we learn to respond intentionally, we reclaim our power over the narrative and ensure our actions align with our purpose. In doing so, we not only lead ourselves with authenticity but also inspire others to respond to their moments with courage and clarity.

So, when your moment comes, take a breath. Remember your response has the power to change trajectory—not just for yourself, but for everyone impacted by your actions. Responding with intention transforms reaction into opportunity, frustration into clarity, and fear into action. It's in these moments that true leadership—and true transformation—is born.

Step 3: Receive the Moment

Acknowledging and responding to a moment is significant, but fully receiving it is where transformation begins. When you receive a moment, it ceases to be an external event and becomes an internal force that empowers you. This step encompasses more than just accepting what life has placed before you. It's embracing it wholeheartedly, with an open heart and a resolute mind. To receive a moment to own it, to let it take root within you, and to allow it to activate the power that already resides within.

Often, we hesitate to fully receive life's pivotal moments because we are shackled by doubt or fear. We question our worthiness, worry about failure, or compare ourselves to others who seem more capable or deserving. But here's the truth: when a moment chooses you, it is not by accident. It is the culmination of all the experiences, lessons, and growth you have undergone up to this point. It is the Creator's way of saying, *You are ready—even if you don't feel it yet.*

When I was thrust into a leadership role during tumultuous times, self-doubt became my unwelcome companion. Could I rise to the occasion? Was I equipped for what lay ahead? Those questions threatened to paralyze me until I chose to reframe them. Instead of asking *Why me?* I began to ask *Why not me?* I realized every trial, every triumph, every moment of preparation had brought me to this place. Receiving that moment wasn't just about stepping into a role—it was about stepping into my purpose.

Receiving the moment means moving beyond recognition of an opportunity to fully internalizing its significance. It is about claiming the power it brings and letting it transform you from the inside out. When you receive, you align with your true self and step into a flow that makes you unstoppable. You walk with a new level of confidence and purpose, no longer held back by hesitation or fear.

To fully receive the moment, you must let go of preconceived notions and lean into the unknown with faith. Release the need to control every detail and trust you are exactly where you are meant to be. Affirm your worth daily. Remind yourself you are capable, deserving, and uniquely positioned to make an impact.

Receiving the moment isn't passive; it is an active choice to lean in with your whole being. It is the moment when the external call to action becomes an internal transformation, where the seeds of potential take root and begin to grow. When you fully receive a moment, you become a force of nature, capable of moving mountains and inspiring others to do the same.

So, when the moment comes, don't just respond—receive it. Take it into your spirit, let it ignite your purpose, and allow it to become the fuel that drives you forward. In receiving, you align with your destiny, and from that alignment comes a power both unstoppable and transformative.

Step 4: Radiate the Moment

The final step in navigating a pivotal moment is to extend its impact beyond yourself. Radiating the moment is more than just sharing the lessons you've learned. It's embodying the transformation you've undergone and allowing it to ripple outward, touching the lives of others in profound and often unseen ways. This step is a commission. It is your moment not only to shine, but to illuminate the paths of those around you, creating a legacy that outlives you.

When you radiate the moment, you move from being a receiver of change to a generator of transformation. Your life becomes a living testimony, a reflection of what is possible when one chooses courage over fear and purpose over hesitation. It is in this act of radiating that your power multiplies, your love expands, and your influence transcends boundaries, reaching hearts and souls far beyond your immediate circle.

When I found my voice and stepped into leadership during the challenges of 2020, I quickly realized my transformation wasn't just for me. It wasn't simply about finding strength to navigate my moment. It was about being entrusted with the responsibility to help others find theirs. Every word I spoke, every decision I made, and every story I shared carried the potential to spark transformation in someone else. I wasn't just leading. I was leaving an imprint on lives I might never meet, and inspiring those who are yet to be born to rise to their own challenges.

Radiating your moment begins with authenticity. By being unapologetically true to yourself, you invite others to do the same. You share your newfound wisdom with an open and generous spirit, recognizing your journey has equipped you with tools that can uplift others. When you radiate, your life radiates hope and inspiration, encouraging others to step into their own power and embrace their moments.

This step also requires intentionality. Your actions, words, and presence carry weight. Use them wisely to create positive change and foster environments where transformation is not only possible but inevitable. By radiating your moment, you become a catalyst for growth, a spark that ignites the hearts of those around you. Your influence expands like ripples in a pond, reaching not only those you directly encounter but also the lives they touch and inspire in turn.

Radiating your moment also means standing as a light in a world that can often feel shrouded in darkness. When you let your light shine unapologetically, it drives out the shadows around you. This light becomes a force of love, hope, and truth, pushing back against the fear, despair, and injustice in the world. You commit to being a source of goodness and refuse to let the darkness encroach on your spirit or dim your purpose.

As you radiate your moment, you align with a divine purpose, one extending beyond what you can see. Your power, once internalized, now flows outward, shaping families, communities, and systems. You begin to impact the world not by imposing change, but by embodying it—showing what is possible when love, courage, and conviction take center stage.

Perhaps the most beautiful truth about radiating your moment is that its effects are eternal. The lives you touch today may inspire generations to come. Your courage to rise, to lead, and to love leaves a legacy transcending time. Even those who are not yet born will feel the waves of transformation set in motion by your willingness to embrace and radiate your moment.

So, when your moment commissions you, don't hold back. Radiate with all the love, power, and purpose within you. Be the light that drives out the darkness, the ripple of change that inspires action, and the catalyst that turns moments into movements. By radiating your moment, you fulfill not only your potential but also the promise of transformation for all who come into your orbit—and beyond.

Summary

In this chapter, "A Moment to Prepare," Coach Charlene emphasizes the importance of preparation for the moments that define our lives. She shares how her dedication to personal development and healing allowed her to respond with clarity and purpose when her moment of calling arrived. The chapter challenges readers to cultivate self-awareness, build resilience, and prepare themselves mentally, emotionally, and spiritually for the opportunities and challenges ahead. It's a call to action to remain ready, to listen to the whispers of purpose, and to step boldly into the moments that shape destiny.

Key Takeaways

- » **Preparation**: Success arises from intentional preparation and being ready to respond when the moment calls.
- » **Courage to Act**: True readiness includes the willingness to act, even when conditions feel imperfect.
- » **Continuous Learning**: Lifelong learning equips us with the tools needed to seize opportunities.

Reflective Questions

1. What areas of your life or career need intentional preparation?
2. How can you overcome fear or hesitation to act when opportunities arise?
3. What skills or knowledge do you need to develop to be ready for your next moment?

Reflective Questions

Reflective Questions

CHAPTER 8

A Moment to Leap

Launching Out into the Deep and Finding Your Destiny

> "Listen to the whispers of your heart, for they are the compass that will guide you to your destiny. Stepping into the unknown may be frightening, but the regret of staying stagnant is far more painful."
>
> —Coach Charlene

The Decision to Leap

After thirty-two years of dedicated service in the healthcare field, I made the profound and challenging decision to retire early and embark on a new chapter in my life. This was not merely a career shift. It was a deliberate leap into the unknown—a journey of self-discovery and alignment with a purpose that had been calling me for years. It wasn't an impulsive decision. It was the culmination of years of whispers from my heart, gently urging me to explore the vastness of my potential.

For the first 18 years of my healthcare career, I thrived. Curiosity drove me, and I was continually learning and developing, finding fulfillment in every challenge. I poured my heart into the work, meeting obstacles with resilience and optimism. But as I approached the eighteen-year mark, something shifted. Those subtle whispers, the gentle nudges from my soul, grew louder. They were telling me something was missing. I tried to silence them, burying them beneath the weight of my responsibilities and the unrelenting grind of my role. But they never left me. They only grew stronger with time.

As I inched closer to retirement, I was filled with excitement at the prospect of finally pursuing the dreams that had been on hold for decades. I envisioned I would be writing, creating, and diving into passion projects that had always taken a backseat. But the reality of stepping into this new chapter wasn't as seamless as I had imagined. Just weeks into my retirement, I found myself inexplicably stuck—unable to fully engage in the pursuits I had longed for. It was as though an invisible barrier stood between me and the freedom I had worked so hard to attain.

Recognizing something was not quite right, I decided to take a thirty-day pause on doing to simply *be*. I decided to walk out into nature, listen to the sounds, and clear my mind. The result of pausing exposed the trauma of years spent striving, ignoring the whispers of my soul, and enduring relentless demands. To move forward, I had to confront the layers of soul pain that had accumulated over years of sacrificing my well-being for the sake of duty.

When I made the commitment to pause, I quickly discovered that even in stillness, my flesh resisted the quiet. It fought to pull me back into the familiar cycle of busyness and striving—a relentless need to prove, to achieve, to stay in motion. This is where my inner coach had to contend with the inner critic that relentlessly whispered, *Keep going, stay busy, don't stop.* That critic thrived on the lie that my worth was tied to my productivity. Yet, as I resisted this urge and leaned into the pause, the truth surfaced: every time I silenced my inner voice, I had unknowingly chipped away at my soul. The result was a pain so deep, so insidious, I hadn't fully recognized its weight until I allowed myself room to feel it. Years of striving to meet organizational demands and personal obligations, all while ignoring my own needs, had left me emotionally exhausted, spiritually drained, and longing for renewal.

The decision to retire was not made lightly. For six years I wrestled with the idea, weighing my options and trying to find ways to stay within the organization that had shaped so much of my professional life. I took on additional assignments, stretching myself across hospital, regional, and national platforms, hoping to align my work with my passion. I created new programs, pitched innovative ideas, and pushed myself to the limit, believing if I just worked harder or contributed more, the right opportunity would come. There were moments when certain opportunities did present themselves—roles that would have advanced my career and positioned me higher within the organization. Yet, every time, there was a hesitation deep within me I couldn't ignore—an inner voice gently urging me to pause instead of stepping forward.

It was in the moment of realization—after years of striving, pushing against the current, and ignoring the whispers of my soul—it finally dawned on me: it was time to leap. This was not a bad realization. It was a powerful nudge, pushing me toward what my heart had been quietly wanting for me all along. The signs had been there, urging me toward a new chapter, but it took those closed doors and my own hesitations to make me see sometimes the next step isn't to stay and try harder. It's to embrace the unknown and step boldly into the future.

It was during this time that these profound words by an anonymous person changed everything for me: "You don't die when your heart stops beating; you die when your heartbeats have no meaning." This truth resonated so deeply it became my North Star. It challenged me to intentionally align my life with what fulfills me. I realized staying where I was, no matter how safe or familiar it felt, was a slow death for my spirit. My heart craved meaning, purpose, and alignment.

Sometimes we stay in places that no longer serve us because we confuse safety with purpose. We convince ourselves we need another job, a new role, or a different title, when in reality the discomfort we feel is the spirit pushing us to grow. Much like the eagle that nudges its fledglings out of the nest, life often requires us to leap before we feel ready. And so, I leapt.

The words from my mentor, Al Hollingsworth, came rushing in during this time, confirming now was the moment to act. His powerful message became another catalyst for this decision: "Charlene, you are trying to swim around in the pool when God is calling you to the ocean, and He wants the ocean to pour back into the pool."

The swimming pool represented my comfort zone—a place of safety, predictability, and limited reach. While it had served me well for years, it could only impact those within its boundaries. The ocean, however, symbolized the expansive possibilities waiting beyond the familiar, teeming with people and opportunities I had yet to touch. This wasn't just about stepping out of my comfort zone. It was about stepping into a calling that demanded I embrace the vast unknown for the sake of all those waiting on the other side of my hesitation.

Those words clarified everything for me—it was time to leave the safety of the familiar and trust the depth and breadth of the purpose that lay ahead. It was no longer about what felt secure. It was about aligning with the larger mission my heart had been yearning for all along.

For the first time in decades, I allowed myself to simply *be*. It was in this stillness clarity emerged, and my next mission was birthed. My soul wasn't just yearning for rest—it was yearning to heal, to create, and to inspire on a scale I had never imagined.

This clarity led to the birth of The Wellness Whisperer Coaching & Consulting LLC, a venture that embodies my purpose. Through this company, I plan to support healthcare workers in reclaiming their well-being, rediscovering their passion, and aligning their lives with their deepest truths. Launching this company hasn't just been a professional pivot—it's been a personal transformation, one that has allowed me to heal, grow, and step into a purpose that feels divinely orchestrated.

This journey has revealed a profound truth: the moments that feel like endings are often disguised beginnings. They are sacred opportunities to realign with our truest selves and to step into a future brimming with possibilities. Leaving the familiar is rarely easy, but it is frequently necessary. It is in the release of what no longer serves us that we make room for what is meant to be.

As I reflect on this path, I am overwhelmed with gratitude—for the challenges that forged my resilience, for the whispers of my soul that refused to be silenced, and for the courage that propelled me to take the leap. This decision, though fraught with uncertainty, has proven to be the most transformative of my life. It has given me the freedom to experience healing in wounds I had ignored for too long, to create in ways I had only dreamed of, and to live with a renewed sense of purpose that transcends anything I had ever experienced.

Now my mission is clear: to help others find their voices, share their stories, and embrace their own moments to leap. Sometimes, staying isn't the answer. Sometimes, the greatest act of courage is to trust the call within, even when it defies logic or challenges comfort. It's daring to believe that on the other side of fear and uncertainty lies the life you were destined to live. Trust the call. Leap boldly into the deep, knowing what awaits is greater than anything you're leaving behind.

In the Valley of Decision

To those standing at the crossroads of uncertainty, carrying the weight of fear and hesitation, I want you to pause and consider this: *What if this is your moment?* As you read these words, as they stir something deep within you, could this be the moment that is choosing you? A persistent discomfort, a gnawing sense of unease, is not a sign of failure—it's your soul's cry for alignment. It's your inner compass, desperately trying to guide you back to the life you were meant to live. The ache you feel is not your enemy, it's a divine nudge, urging you to step out of the shadows and into your purpose.

Yes, the unknown feels daunting. The fear of failure, rejection, or even success can feel overwhelming. It's easy to convince yourself you have nothing special to offer, your voice doesn't matter, or the world will keep spinning without your contribution. But let me tell you something: *what you carry within you is irreplaceable.* It is unique, and it is desperately needed. The world is waiting—not for perfection, but for your authenticity, your story, your gifts.

For those of you in your current roles, feeling a sense of fulfillment and purpose, this moment may still be calling you. Not to leave, but to level up. To step into an even greater version of yourself. Is there a program you've dreamed of creating, a team culture you've envisioned improving, or a way to use your knowledge and creativity to enhance patient care, workplace harmony, or innovation in your field? The human spirit thrives on challenges stretch us, ignite our gifts and passions. If you've felt a tug to do more, to grow, or to make a lasting impact, don't ignore it. This could be your moment to rise to the next level and leave an indelible mark on your environment.

I'm not asking you to quit your job or abandon your responsibilities. What I am asking is that you listen. Quiet the noise, hush the doubts, and tune into the whisper of your soul. That whisper is sacred. It's your roadmap, the voice that knows your deepest desires and the steps you need to take. It's not demanding a reckless leap, it's inviting a courageous, intentional movement toward a life that feels like yours.

Fear will try to anchor you to the familiar, but staying stuck comes at a cost—a life of unfulfilled potential and lingering regret. Imagine looking back years from now and realizing you allowed fear to silence your dreams, to rob the world of your impact. The pain of staying stuck far outweighs the uncertainty of stepping forward.

So, my challenge to you is this: *What will you do when the moment chooses you?* Because perhaps, right now as you read this, the moment is here. It's calling your name, asking you to step forward, to rise, to trust. Chart your course one step at a time. Start small if you must, but start. Trust that the same voice calling you forward will also guide and equip you. The time is now—not tomorrow, not next year, but *now*. Don't let this moment slip away. You are capable. You are worthy. And whether it's time to pivot or level up, your destiny is waiting for you to claim it.

Summary

Chapter 8, "A Moment to Leap," invites readers to step beyond the boundaries of comfort and familiarity to embrace the transformative power of bold action. Coach Charlene shares how her decision to take a leap of faith was rooted in trusting her inner calling, even when the path ahead seemed uncertain. By confronting fear and doubt, she found the courage to pursue her purpose and create a ripple effect of impact.

This chapter emphasizes that stepping into your destiny often requires leaving behind what is safe and known. It challenges readers to trust the process, lean into their faith, and embrace discomfort as a necessary part of growth. Ultimately, it's a reminder that true transformation happens when we dare to leap, trusting the net will appear and the journey will lead us to our greatest potential.

Key Takeaways

- » **Taking Risks**: Bold actions often lead to the most profound outcomes.
- » **Faith and Trust:** Trusting your instincts and taking leaps of faith are essential to discovering our destiny.
- » **Resilience in Uncertainty**: Even when the path is unclear, resilience will guide us through the unknown.

Reflective Questions

1. What risks are you currently avoiding that could lead to significant growth?
2. How can you cultivate faith in your abilities and trust in the process?
3. What role does resilience play in navigating uncertainty in your journey?

Reflective Questions

Reflective Questions

CHAPTER 9

A Moment to Share

Wisdom Jewel from a Black Nurse Leader's Journey

Everyone's journey and path will be different.

But remember, many of the challenges we experience become the spark igniting the fires of innovation and creativity. I have learned every experience, whether bathed in the light of joy or shrouded in the shadows of adversity, serves a purpose, guiding us toward our destined path. Through the pages of *When the Moment Chooses You*, I've traversed valleys of potential despair and scaled peaks of triumph, discovering within every trial lies the seed of purpose waiting to be unearthed. For it is through adversity that we cultivate resilience, through sorrow that we nurture empathy, and through challenges that we forge our character. Each faith journey, each encounter—whether serendipitous or difficult—shapes the intricate design of our lives, leading us powerfully toward our destiny.

As we bid farewell to these pages, let us carry forward this understanding: every experience, no matter how seemingly insignificant, is a thread woven into the fabric of our existence. Embrace the journey, for within its trials and triumphs lies the essence of our being, calling us to seize each moment with courage, gratitude, and an unwavering belief in the transformative power of the human spirit.

I leave you with one final offering—a Wisdom Jewel. This is not just an insight, but a deeply personal reflection, a love letter to those who, like me, have walked through doors where their voices were not always welcomed; where their presence was questioned; where their brilliance was overlooked. This is for every trailblazer who has ever felt alone.

A Letter to My Black and Brown Trailblazers

Dear Beloved Trailblazers,

To all who have walked through spaces where your brilliance was overlooked, your voice was silenced, and your presence was diminished—this is for you. To those who have faced the sting of invisibility, the weight of rejection, and the ache of isolation, I need you to hear this: **I see you. I hear you. I value you.**

I know the courage it takes to navigate a world that often seems indifferent to your struggles. The resilience required to stand tall amid microaggressions, systemic racism, and the exhausting pressure to prove yourself can feel overwhelming. Yet, here you are—still showing up, still shining, still rising. Your authenticity in the face of a world that tries to diminish your light is nothing short of revolutionary.

But I also know the pain that comes with carrying these burdens in silence. The moments when you've questioned whether anyone really understands the weight you bear. The feeling of being unseen and unheard can be crushing, and I want you to know this: *you are not alone.*

You are part of a legacy of strength, a lineage of warriors and trailblazers who have overcome unimaginable odds. Your existence is a testament to the power of resilience, and your journey is not in vain. The road may be lonely at times, but your footsteps are creating pathways for those who will come after you. Your light is illuminating spaces that desperately need change, even when it feels like the world doesn't notice.

I write this letter not only to affirm your worth but to extend an invitation: *reach out.* You don't have to carry this alone. There are people who see you, who care about your well-being, and who want to support you. Whether it's a mentor, a friend, or a community of like-minded individuals, seek out those places where you can share your story and let your guard down. Healing happens in community.

I also hope this letter serves as a call to inspire you to *find your voice* and impact those around you. As author Dianna Hardy said, "One voice at the right pitch can create an avalanche." I had no idea finding my own voice and using it for change would spread out and touch so many lives. What started as a simple act of courage turned into a movement that uplifted not just me, but countless others who needed to hear a voice that resonated with their own struggles and hopes.

Your voice, too, carries immense power. It has the ability to challenge, to disrupt, to heal, and to transform. Even if it feels small at first, your voice can create waves of change that extend far beyond what you can see. Let this moment be your invitation to speak up, to take action, and inspire those around you.

Let me remind you of this power you carry. The stories you hold, the perspective you bring, and the gifts you share are irreplaceable. Your presence has the ability to transform rooms, challenge systems, and inspire others to find their own courage. You are a trailblazer, paving the way for a world that is more just, more unified, and more compassionate.

Even in the moments when you feel unseen, remember this: *your impact is immeasurable.* Every time you show up as your true self, you are planting seeds of change. Every time you speak up, you are challenging the status quo. And every time you persevere, you are proving love, resilience, and authenticity can overcome even the most entrenched barriers.

I am proud of you. I am inspired by you. And I stand with you. Together, we are part of a larger movement—a collective force for good that is rewriting narratives, breaking chains, and creating a future where every voice is heard, and every life is valued.

If you take nothing else from this letter, let it be this: *you are not alone, and you are deeply loved.* Your journey matters, and so do you. Keep rising, keep shining, and know the world is better because you are in it.

With unwavering love, solidarity, and hope,
Charlene Johnson
Your Sister on the Journey

As we reflect on the journey, it's clear the path forward is not without its challenges. Yet within every challenge lies an opportunity—a chance to rise, to speak, and to create change. The letter serves as a reminder you are not alone in this journey, *but it also calls you to action.* To build on this foundation, I offer the following key messages as guiding principles. They are meant to inspire, empower, and equip you to take the next step with courage and purpose. Let these messages ignite the fire within you to find your voice, embrace your humanity, and lean into the strength of collective action.

Key Messages from the Book

1. Finding Your Voice

Your voice is your power, and the world desperately needs to hear it. Finding your voice means more than just speaking—it is reclaiming your narrative, owning your value, and standing firm in your truth. It is using your experiences, your perspective, and your story to inspire and ignite change.

Yes, there will be moments when staying silent feels easier. But silence won't bring the change you seek, and it won't honor the resilience you've cultivated. Speaking up takes courage. Especially where you feel unseen or unheard. But courage is transformative—not just for you, but for those who witness it. Share your story boldly, knowing it has the power to challenge the status quo and spark a movement.

Remember: the echo of your voice is not only for yourself—it reverberates for those who haven't yet found their voice. Be the light that shows others the way.

2. It's Okay Not to Be Okay

Let me say it again: it is **okay not to be okay**. It's okay to feel tired, to feel overwhelmed, to feel like you've reached your limit. These feelings are not signs of weakness. They are evidence of your humanity. Acknowledge them. Sit with them. Let them remind you of the strength it takes to keep going. But don't stay in isolation with those feelings. Reach out. Share your struggles with a trusted community, whether it's a friend, a mentor, or a group of like-minded individuals.

Vulnerability is not a sign of defeat. It is the starting point for healing. In sharing your burdens, you make way for others to carry them with you.

Together, you create a foundation for resilience and renewal. Give yourself permission to rest, to recover, and lean on those who are ready to hold you up. You are not meant to do this alone.

3. Embrace Collective Strength

Nature offers us profound wisdom. Birds fly in a V formation not by accident, but by design. They take turns leading and following, sharing the effort, and drawing strength from one another. This is the power of collective strength. We are not meant to journey alone. Our power grows exponentially when we lean on one another, when we create margin for collaboration, mutual support, and shared leadership. There innovation thrives, and solutions emerge.

When you feel isolated, remember this: there is a community waiting to support you. Lean into that strength, and let your presence be a pillar for others. Together, we can break barriers, dismantle inequalities, and forge paths where none existed before.

Be Bold Enough to Reach Out

Reaching out can feel daunting, especially when trust has been broken or your voice has been dismissed in the past. But connection is often the catalyst for healing and transformation. Your growth and empowerment begin when you allow others to see you, hear you, and walk alongside you.

- » Seek out mentors to guide you, sponsors to advocate for you, and allies to stand with you.
- » Build relationships with people who recognize your worth and are willing to invest in your journey. These connections don't just uplift you. They create a network of support that amplifies your impact.
- » Don't be afraid to ask for help, to seek guidance, or to offer your own hand to someone else. Vulnerability and connection are the bedrock of progress and belonging.

Summary

Chapter 9, "A Moment to Share," serves as a heartfelt offering of wisdom from Coach Charlene's deep desire to give back and be part of the solution. Despite the personal pain, invisible scars, and challenges she endured as a Black nurse leader navigating systemic racism, Coach Charlene chose to transform her experiences into tools of empowerment. This chapter reflects her unwavering commitment to share her journey—not out of obligation, but from a profound place of love and purpose. This chapter is a call to action, a bridge to understanding, and a pathway to hope for anyone seeking to create lasting impact in their personal or professional lives.

Leadership with purpose requires intentionality, a commitment to listening, and a deep respect for the humanity of everyone in the room. As we close this chapter, remember the power of sharing lies in its ability to connect, inspire, and transform. It is through these moments of vulnerability and courage that true leadership is born. Together, let's continue to build a world where every voice is valued, every story is honored, and every individual has the opportunity to thrive.

Key Takeaways

- » **Amplify Voices**: Sharing our story empowers others to find their own voices.
- » **Community and Solidarity:** Collective strength amplifies individual efforts, creating an ongoing effect of change.
- » **Inclusive Leadership**: Fostering diversity, equity, and belonging makes it possible for all to flourish.
- » **Bonus Takeaway—the Power of Reflection**: Considering our journey reveals lessons to inspire and guide others.

Reflective Questions

1. How can sharing your story inspire others to step into their purpose?
2. What steps can you take to build solidarity and collaboration within your team or community?
3. How can you incorporate inclusive leadership practices into your professional life?
4. Bonus Reflective Question—what lessons from your journey can be shared to empower the next generation of leaders?

Reflective Questions

Reflective Questions

A Final Word from Coach Charlene

Find Your Voice and Unleash Your Impact

One of the most profound moments in my journey was when I found my voice. This wasn't just about speaking words. I stepped into the fullness of my purpose, embraced the power within me to create change, and responded boldly to the moment that chose me. When I found my voice, something shifted inside. I became unstoppable. That voice gave me the confidence to speak up, even in the face of discomfort, fear, or resistance. It wasn't just about being heard—it was about standing firmly for what is right and inspiring others to do the same.

Your voice is more than just a tool for expression—it is a vessel for your experiences, wisdom, and passion. It carries the weight of your unique journey, and when you use it with intention, it can move mountains. Even when I knew I was misaligned in some areas of my professional life, my voice allowed me to make a difference right where I was. I used it to create room for dialogue, to challenge the status quo, and to be an advocate for those who felt unseen and unheard. In doing so, I learned a powerful truth: you don't have to be perfectly aligned with your ultimate purpose to make an impact. Wherever you are right now, your voice can light the way for others.

Finding your voice is more than simply speaking—you welcome the power within you to influence change. You move boldly into your role as a lifeline of hope and a catalyst for transformation. Your voice has the power to challenge injustices, dismantle barriers, and inspire positive change that continues to grow. It can transform your life and the lives of those who hear it.

When you find your voice, you unapologetically accept your authentic self. You become a source of light for others, showing them adversity can be overcome, and one person can make a profound difference. The impact of your voice doesn't stop with you—it multiplies, creating a movement toward fulfillment, justice, and belonging.

Never underestimate the importance of your voice.

This is your moment—perhaps the one you've been waiting for. Don't let fear or doubt silence you. Acknowledge your power. Speak your truth. Watch as your voice creates waves of impact far beyond what you could ever imagine.

Together we will create a world where every voice is valued, every individual has the opportunity to thrive, and every challenge is met with courage and resilience.

Your destiny is calling. Answer it with all your heart.

Conclusion

For too long, silence has been the enemy of progress. It has stifled voices, perpetuated injustices, and dimmed the light of countless individuals who longed to make a difference. But the time for silence is over. As we stand at this pivotal moment in history, we are called to break free from the chains of fear, to speak truth to power, and to illuminate the path forward with courage, compassion, and collective resolve.

It is not the challenges we encounter that define us, but how we choose to respond to them. Will you shrink back, or will you rise? Will you let fear hold you captive, or will you move boldly into the unknown? The moment that chooses you will not wait. It demands your courage, your voice, and your unwavering belief in the possibility of change.

I ask you this: *What will you do when the moment chooses you?*

Will you seize it with all your heart, letting it transform not only your life but the lives of those around you?

The time is now.

The world is waiting for your voice, your courage, and your unique contribution. Step forward. Let your light shine! Together, we can create a legacy that echoes through generations—a legacy of hope, healing, and boundless possibility.

Step Into Your Moment

Your journey doesn't stop here. Let's take the next step together.

At The Wellness Whisperer Coaching & Consulting, we recognize the deep challenges healthcare professionals and leaders face daily—burnout, exhaustion, disconnection from purpose, and the struggle to maintain well-being while serving others.

I created this space to help you reclaim your joy, restore balance, and lead with heart. If you've felt unseen, overworked, or unsure of your next steps, know that transformation is possible.

Problems We Solve at The Wellness Whisperer

- ✔ Chronic stress and burnout that lead to emotional exhaustion
- ✔ Feeling unseen, undervalued, or disconnected from purpose
- ✔ Struggling to maintain well-being while navigating workplace demands
- ✔ Transitioning from burnout to a more fulfilling career or leadership role
- ✔ Helping leaders and teams build resilience, well-being, and a healthy workplace culture

Ways to Work With Me

- » **ICU Experience**
  A transformative workshop designed to help healthcare professionals and leaders heal, engage, and thrive in their personal and professional lives.

- » **The Recovery Room**
  A healing experience for those who left their workplace due to exhaustion, transitioned to something new, or retired early and are seeking renewal and clarity.

- » **The Birthing Room Experience**
  A space for individuals ready to birth new ideas, projects, or transitions, modeled after the labor and delivery process—nurturing, pushing through challenges, and delivering something meaningful.

- » **Personalized Coaching for Healthcare Professionals & Organizations**
  One-on-one and organizational coaching designed to help professionals build resilience, reignite their purpose, and create a culture of well-being and sustainable success.

- » **Speaking & Workshops**
  I provide keynotes, training, and interactive sessions on well-being, resilience, leadership, and workplace healing for healthcare teams, organizations, and conferences.

- » **Coaching & Consulting**
  Strategic consulting and coaching tailored to organizations seeking to integrate well-being initiatives, leadership development, and cultural transformation into their workplace.

Let's Start the Conversation

Contact me at: info@wellnesswhispererconsulting.com
Learn more: wellnesswhispererconsulting.com

Your moment is now. Let's step into it together!

About the Author

Charlene Johnson

A Visionary Leader in Healthcare Well-being

Charlene Johnson, MSN, RN, Caritas Coach, HeartMath Trainer, is the visionary founder of The Wellness Whisperer Coach & Consulting LLC, dedicated to transforming the well-being of healthcare professionals. With over thirty years' experience in nursing, leadership, and academia, Charlene has turned defining moments into transformative movements. She specializes in *Caring Science* integration, *HeartMath* training, and leadership development.

As a professor, she is passionate about educating and mentoring the next generation of nurses and leaders. She ensures they prioritize well-being, resilience, and compassionate care from the beginning of their careers. Her decision to retire early and launch this initiative was fueled by a deep commitment to healthcare workers still navigating the emotional toll of burnout, workplace dissatisfaction, and post-pandemic trauma. Through coaching, speaking engagements, and consulting work, Charlene empowers individuals and organizations to reclaim joy, resilience, and purpose in their work, fostering compassionate, high-quality care for both providers and patients.

Charlene is also the host of two transformative shows: *When the Moment Chooses You,* a podcast where she interviews experts, trailblazers, and change agents who have stepped into their calling, and *The Whispers of Wellness,* a show dedicated to prioritizing well-being and creating sustainable self-care practices. Through these platforms, she amplifies voices that spark change and shares strategies that empower others to thrive.

A sought-after speaker, master motivator, and compassionate facilitator, Charlene is known for her ability to spark lasting change. She helps people find their voice so they embrace their impact and lead with intention. Her work is a testament to the power of love, determination, and purpose-driven leadership. She is a guiding force who equips healthcare professionals and future leaders with the tools they need to thrive—one heartbeat, one moment, and one movement at a time.

With Love and Appreciation!

Dear Reader,

From the depths of my heart, thank you. Thank you for choosing to take this journey with me, for allowing my words to meet you in the spaces where you needed them most. Writing *When the Moment Chooses You* has been a deeply personal and transformative experience—one that I poured my heart and soul into, knowing that somewhere, someone like you was meant to receive it.

This is my first solo book, and to have you reading it means more than I can express. Your presence here is no accident. The fact that you picked up this book tells me you, too, are being called to something greater. A powerful part of you waits to be unleashed. Your life has meaning. Your story is not over. And as long as you are here on this earth, there is purpose in your existence.

One of the biggest joys of my life is to inspire others to see their own greatness. You carry an extraordinary quality within you—something the world needs. My hope is that this book has awakened a new level of awareness in you, a reminder that your voice, your presence, and your purpose matter more than you know.

Your support throughout this process has been invaluable, and I am incredibly grateful for you. If this book has spoken to you, I would be honored if you could take a moment to leave a review on Amazon. Your thoughts and feedback not only mean the world to me but also help others decide if this book might be the encouragement they need on their own journey.

With deep gratitude,
Coach Charlene

Heartfelt Gratitude to Robin and Lisa

As I reflect on the journey of bringing *When the Moment Chooses You* to life, I am overwhelmed with gratitude for two extraordinary women who played an instrumental role in making this vision a reality—Robin, my incredible editor, and Lisa Peterson, my brilliant Creative Director at Bookable Media.

Robin, your keen attention to detail, compassionate listening, and unwavering dedication ensured that every word in this book carried the depth and power it was meant to. But beyond your skill, there is an anointing on your work—one that goes beyond editing and into the realm of divine alignment. You didn't just refine my words; you honored the spirit behind them, allowing this book to breathe with authenticity, power, and grace.

Lisa, your creative brilliance and visionary approach took this project to heights beyond what I imagined. You saw the heart of this book and transformed it into a work of art—one that speaks, inspires, and moves people. Your ability to turn vision into reality is nothing short of extraordinary.

I could not have done this without the two of you. Thank you for your passion, your excellence, and for believing in this message as much as I do. Because of you, *When the Moment Chooses You* is not just a book—it's a movement.

With deep gratitude,
Coach Charlene

When Silence is No Longer Safety

There comes a time when silence is no longer safety
When stillness is no longer peace
A time when the weight of unspoken truths
Presses too heavily against the soul.

The moment will come—unexpected, undeniable
It will not knock softly
It will not wait for permission
It will rise like a tide
Pulling you toward something greater than yourself.

Will you answer?

Will you rise from the quiet corners
Where fear once held you hostage?
Will you let your voice carve new pathways
Through the walls that once confined you?

Strength is not the absence of fear
It is standing in its presence
Choosing courage anyway
It is speaking when your voice shakes
Moving forward when your legs tremble
Believing in the unseen
Trusting in the call.

The world is waiting
Not for perfect words
Not for certainty
But for you
For the fire in your spirit
For the wisdom in your scars
For the power that lives in your truth.

So, when the moment chooses you—**stand**
When the world calls your name—**speak**
When destiny reaches for your hand—**take it**
Because your story is not just yours
It is a light, a guide, a revolution waiting to unfold.

This is your moment
Step forward
Rise
Transform
Let the echoes of your courage
Become the anthem of those still searching for their voice.

Made in the USA
Columbia, SC
01 May 2025